PATHWAYS TO PLAY

Sandra Heidemann and Deborah Hewitt

Redleaf Press
a division of Resources for Child Caring

Photographs: Bm Porter/Don Franklin – Cover, 14, 34, 48, 52, 63, 73, 77, 89
Michael Siluk – Cover, 9, 21, 40, 58, 67, 82
Francis Wardle – Cover, 26

ISBN: 0-934140-65-0

Published by: Redleaf Press
Formerly Toys 'n Things Press
a division of Resources for Child Caring
450 North Syndicate, Suite 5
St. Paul, Minnesota 55104

Distributed by: Gryphon House
PO Box 275
Mt. Rainier, Maryland 20712

Library of Congress Cataloging-in-Publication Data

Heidemann, Sandra, 1946-
Pathways to play : developing play skills in young children / by Sandra Heidemann, Debbie Hewitt.
p. cm.
ISBN: 0-934140-65-0
1. Play. 2. Education, Preschool. 3. Child development.
I. Hewitt, Debbie, 1958- . II. Title.
LB1137.H38 1992
155.4'18–dc20 92-17167 CIP

TABLE OF CONTENTS

PREFACE

This book began as a simple idea. We wanted to design a play checklist that would help caregivers observe children's play skills. Little did we know that this simple idea would take so much work and time and yield such worthwhile results.

The need for a checklist was apparent to both of us as teachers and child care consultants. Often we would sit with a beleaguered caregiver and hear stories of a child that was aggressive, defiant, volatile, and anxious. Inevitably, the caregiver would also state that the child did not play with other children. We could help the caregiver reduce the aggression with a behavior management plan but this did not help the child participate more in play. We felt a checklist could help a caregiver pinpoint the play skills that need work and plan goals for improving those play skills.

We began a long search for the right instrument to give caregivers. We used Smilansky's Play Inventory (1968) to help caregivers understand the complex variables of sociodramatic play. However, the Inventory didn't give caregivers a good picture of the child's social skills, i.e., how the child entered a play group or how he handled conflict. Other play assessments were lengthy and assessed the developmental age of the child's play. We wanted an instrument that was relatively short and that caregivers could use easily in their setting. Also this instrument didn't need to assess the developmental level of play. It was needed more as a tool to observe play and to use in planning appropriate goals. This meant it had to be short, pertinent, and easy to understand.

We decided to develop a checklist that would address both sociodramatic play skills and social skills. The process of designing the checklist proved to be longer and more laborious than originally planned. There were countless revisions as colleagues and caregivers gave us valuable feedback.

After finishing the Play Checklist, we presented it to many caregivers in workshops and individual consultations. Invariably, the feedback has been positive and enthusiastic. To further help caregivers in their planning, we added suggestions and activities to do with children who are learning play skills. Caregivers report that not only has the information helped them plan for the child that is having difficulty with cooperative play, but it has also helped them understand the complexity that makes play the wonder that it is.

We hope you will find the Play Checklist and our suggestions for activities useful and interesting. We also wish for you many playful times as you care for those who teach us the most about play: the children.

INTRODUCTION

We wrote this book to help caregivers focus on children's play skills. Play skills are vital to a child's overall healthy development. Play teaches children about symbols, solving conflict, and taking turns. Learning how to play with others is the foundation for interacting with others through grade school and into adulthood. However, the training many caregivers receive may not include extensive information on play skills. We assume that a child will gain these skills naturally. We are more likely to work on language and cognitive skills in our settings. It is true that most children do learn to play in a group with only a little facilitation by adults, but it is also true that there are children who do not acquire the skills naturally. These children may be very withdrawn or very aggressive. They may stand outside the group casting longing glances or push to enter a group. Often these children are the ones with difficult emotional issues in their families: abuse and neglect, chemical dependency, divorce, separation and loss, and trauma of many kinds (Irwin, 1983). If you can help these children play successfully, you are giving them a gift for life.

We divided the book into chapters that correspond to the process you will use as you plan experiences to teach play skills.

Chapter 1 reviews the definitions of the terms we will use throughout the book. We outline how play helps a child begin to use symbols and to interact with other children.

Chapter 2 gives suggestions for enhancing the play already occurring in the setting.

Chapter 3 presents the Play Checklist and guidelines for observation. The chapter highlights our Play Checklist and gives you a picture of how each item matches a child's skill.

Chapters 4 and 5 move into how you plan from the checklist. We discuss goals, priorities, and the role of the adult.

Chapter 6 is filled with suggestions for improving the play skills that correspond with each section of the checklist.

Chapter 7 discusses evaluation and the crucial role it plays in successful planning.

Appendix 1 outlines a few reasons why children may have difficulty learning play skills.

Appendix 2 is included for those of you who would like to teach the content of this book to other caregivers.

As we worked on this book, we drew from Sara Smilansky's (1968) material. Parts of the checklist and many of the concepts present began with her work. We acknowledge and appreciate her pioneering work on children's play.

Because we do not want to exclude either boys or girls, we have chosen to use the pronouns "he" and "she" in alternating chapters. For the adult working with the children, we use the term "caregiver" because it best describes the wide variety of people caring for children.

We are indebted to the Washburn Child Guidance Center, the Greater Minneapolis Day Care Association, and the Southside Family Nurturing Center for the experiences and learning opportunities that formed the basis for this book. The many children, families, caregivers, and fellow staff we worked with while at these agencies helped us to formulate the ideas put forth here. We would like to thank the people who took our workshops and classes and challenged us with questions that clarified our views. A special thanks to Terry Halfin for her permission to use her case study as an example. We are grateful to our readers Jim Stengel, Jeff Hewitt, Diane McLinn, and Caroline Winget for the many thoughtful insights that helped to strengthen the manuscript. We also appreciate the patience and confidence of our editor, Eileen Nelson, as we attempted to put our thoughts into words.

Writing a book while working at other jobs is a challenging task. A very heartfelt thank-you goes to our husbands, Jim and Jeff, and our children, Carrie, Daniel, and Marcia. Our children provided many examples, inspiration, and greatly needed humor. Our husbands took on more than their fair share of household tasks, listened to partially-formed ideas, and supported us at every juncture.

CHAPTER 1

THE BASICS OF PLAY

Andrea busily arranges boxes, clothes, and blankets as she lets others know, "This is where we keep our money and other things, too." Timmy uses a sweet, high voice and answers, "I'll get the babies over here." He hands a doll to Lisa. She lays it on a blanket and declares, "This is where we change the diapers." Andrea quickly moves the doll off the blanket and says, "No! This is a mattress, not a changing pad."

Timmy hands another doll to Lisa as he explains, "Oh, oh! I left my baby out here. You take her." Once free of the doll he spins in a circle and shrieks in a gruff, low voice, "I get some magical powers and can fly. When you're up here you just turn around."

Andrea ignores Timmy, looks over her house and states, "Our house is turning out nice." Lisa agrees, "Andrea knows how to clean up a mess. Don't you think so, Timmy?" Timmy stops spinning and suggests, "Let's pretend it's night now." The three of them settle onto the blanket and close their eyes.

The animated and imaginative play of Andrea, Timmy, and Lisa is woven together as they create their story. They are engaged in a complex level of play in which they combine the use of objects, actions, verbalizations, and interactions into a sociodramatic play scene. When you think about play you might visualize one child sitting in a sandbox patting mudpies, a couple of children putting on dress-up clothes and make-up to get ready to go out, or a group of children gathering blocks, pegs, and puzzle pieces as the ingredients for the soup they have bubbling on the stove. The foundations of sociodramatic play, the most complex form of play, lie in how children use objects and how they interact with one another in play. Because of the intricacies of play, adults have spent many hours discussing and researching it. From this study comes an impressive body of knowledge that helps us learn about a child's play. In this first chapter, we review and define types of play:

Play with Objects
Social Play
Sociodramatic Play

PLAY WITH OBJECTS

Play in the early childhood years is often centered around the use of objects. The way in which a child uses objects in play changes with her maturity and her ability to pretend. When a child first plays with a new toy she spends time exploring the object physically. She uses her senses to discover how the object works and what she might do with it. A child with a brightly colored Lego building block will turn it over and over to examine all of its sides. She may stick her fingers in the holes of the Lego block or feel the rise of the bumps. After exploring it the child may use the Lego block to play hiding games or to bang it on the bottom of a pan. When she is capable of fitting them together she may begin to build by stacking Lego blocks on top of one another. With practice, her building will become more skilled and she may try to make one of the cars pictured in the Lego pamphlet. At another time, when she is pretending to be in a rock band, she may return to the box of Lego blocks to look for something that can become a microphone. Yet another day, Lego blocks may become the place markers for a game of hopscotch.

Children tend to use materials in the ways described above. First they use their senses to explore and learn about an object; then to see how it fits with other objects and to build with it; then objects become props for pretend play; and finally materials are incorporated into the games children play. The types of play in which children engage while using objects have been outlined below.

Sensorimotor Play

Sensorimotor play refers to the activity a child does when she learns to use her muscles through repetitive movements. Infants spend many of their waking hours in sensorimotor play. You see them explore objects by turning them, pressing, poking, and prodding. Toddlers demonstrate their sensorimotor skills when they dump out toys or practice jumping. Preschoolers engage in this form of play when stirring sand, patting playdough, or pouring water.

Constructive Play

Hunter, a five-year-old boy, took several chunks of playdough the size of robins' eggs and began rolling

Michael Siluk

them into balls. He asked for toothpicks, which he stuck into the balls at various places. Finally, he connected the balls with drinking straws and announced he had built the "borf molecule." Hunter is engaged in constructive play; he uses materials to make or build things.

Construction may begin at a very simple level as when a twelve month old places one block on top of another, or a toddler stacks ten blocks in a tower. As the child's skills improve, she may show her ability to balance her design and use materials to duplicate a building or a molecule as Hunter had done. Other materials like Tinker Toy blocks, Lego blocks, playdough, and markers might be used by a child in construction.

Dramatic Play

Dramatic play involves two skills: representational skills, when a child begins to use objects to pretend, and role-playing, when the child takes on a pretend role.

A. Representational Skills

The ability to understand that one item may represent another, referred to as a representational skill, is closely related to a child's overall cognitive development (Vygotsky, 1976; Golomb, 1979). As a child matures she is able to think more abstractly (Piaget, 1962), and a symbol or a replica of an object can take the place of the real object for the child. The ways in which a child uses objects to represent others corresponds to this cognitive maturation (Wolfgang, Mackender, & Wolfgang, 1981).

Young children need to use a real object or an exact replica of the object in their play. For instance, in pretending to diaper a doll, an eighteen-month-old child would do best using a real diaper. Shortly after a child turns two she may be able to use a substitute or a similar object to pretend. A replica of a diaper, such as a doll's diaper, might be used by a child at this level. When a child is around three years of age, materials further from the real object might be substituted in play. In the diapering example, a child at this level might use a tissue as a diaper. At four years, a child may be capable of pretending to diaper with no diaper at all. This demonstrates that she is able to think more abstractly than before since she is now able to let her actions take the place of a real object.

B. Role-Playing

Role-playing is also an important part of dramatic play. Children role play when they use materials, voice, and actions to imitate others during play (Wolfgang, Mackender, & Wolfgang, 1981). When a child first learns to role play she takes on familiar roles like parent or doctor. She uses the materials they would use as props to support her actions. For instance, she may use a cylinder block as a syringe when pretending to be a doctor. As she becomes familiar with other people and their roles, she may imitate the actions and verbalizations of a grocer, waitress, or firefighter. Playing fantasy characters like monster, Cinderella, or super hero become common as a child is able to engage in more abstract thinking.

Games with Rules

Children play games with rules at all ages. The games and rules change as the child grows older. Infants play games like peek-a-boo or "drop the toy off the high chair tray." Toddlers enjoy games of chase and preschoolers begin to do well with simple board games.

At whatever age, games have rules that are agreed upon by all players. Rules help to organize play and allow it to continue. Sometimes the rules are established prior to the game as they might be in a board game. Simple games with rules include pat-a-cake, lotto, and tag. More complicated games with rules are Candyland, Chutes and Ladders, and dodge ball. In all games, if the rules are not agreed upon and followed by all the players,conflict develops quickly and play may fall apart.

Understanding the many ways children use materials in play is vital to understanding their play. The following chart summarizes the different types of play with objects:

PLAY WITH OBJECTS		
TYPE OF PLAY	**USE OF OBJECT**	**EXAMPLES**
Sensorimotor	Explores properties of object by banging, stirring, rolling, etc.	Banging pots and pans Making mud pies
Constructive	Uses materials to make or build things	Using all types of blocks and toys to build towers, buildings, enclosures, etc.
Dramatic	Uses objects to pretend Begins with real objects Acts out roles using imaginary objects	Playing house, restaurant, or doctor
Games with rules	Games are played with shared rules Rules can be unspoken or formally stated	Playing peek-a-boo, chase, Candyland, or Chutes and Ladders

Adapted from McNellis, Ed., 1987.

SOCIAL PLAY

As children play, they come into contact with other children as well as with objects. To play successfully with others, children must learn to coordinate their behaviors and to cooperate. Children must learn the give-and-take patterns of social play. Social play can be grouped into five different types of play, based on the interactions that happen during the play (Parten, 1932).

Play with Adults

Play with others usually begins with adult/child interactions. Very young infants play games with their parents as they coo back and forth to one another. Or the adult may begin to play by blowing a bubble and pausing for a response. The child may laugh or blow a bubble back and the game starts over again. The interactions are usually repetitious and this rhythmic interaction between the adult and child helps to establish a conversational tone. This is viewed by some as the beginnings of turn-taking (Mac Donald and Gillette, 1985). Other examples of typical play between infants and adults include peek-a-boo, "so big," and pat-a-cake.

Solitary Play

Jose brought his caregiver blocks to stack. He watched expectantly as the tower grew taller and taller. After ten blocks were stacked, he could stand it no longer and gleefully kicked them over. Gabriel was nearby. He picked up snap-together beads and put them in a carton. He glanced frequently in Jose's direction but did not attempt to join his play. This type of solitary play is what you see when watching a twelve to eighteen month old. Children this age usually play alone rather than with their peers. The presence of an adult is often needed to ensure the continuation of play. Children gain approval and a sense of security from the adult's presence, attention, and comments.

Children at this age watch and enjoy the activity of others. However, they have not yet learned to coordinate their behaviors so that they are able to play together. When infants do interact, the interaction is usually very brief and most often comes about because both children want the same toy at the same time (Rubin, 1980). Infants may also interact with one another by touching, poking, or prodding. Usually the child is trying to learn about this other creature in the same physically explorative way she learns about the rest of the world (Rubin, 1980). You need a watchful eye at these times as the exploration can all too quickly become hair-pulling or pinching.

Parallel Play

Between the ages of two and two and a half, play changes and you begin to see children playing nearer to one another. Parallel play is characterized by the way the children play side by side with very little exchange of materials or conversation. At this level, the activities of the children are likely to be unrelated. For instance, while sitting next to one another one child may be talking on a toy telephone while another is building with blocks. You might also see parallel play where a number of children are playing in the housekeeping corner, all pretending to cook, but not exchanging any ideas or conversation. Children engaging in parallel play like being near each other but are not ready for coordinated interactions.

Associative Play

A group of children were seated at a table and they were all using playdough. Ernie rolled ropes, Theresa used the rolling pin to flatten out pancakes, and Destry patted the dough until it was flat enough to cut with a cookie cutter. When Theresa saw Ernie use scissors to cut his rope into pretend pieces of candy, she abandoned her rolling pin and began to roll ropes too. A few minutes later she searched for scissors and cut her ropes into small pieces. This is associative play. At two and a half or three, children begin to like playing in groups that are involved in the same activity. The children tend to watch one another and to imitate the actions of their peers, but verbal exchanges are limited. They borrow materials and ideas from one another but they don't work together to create. A child might look over to see what her neighbor is building, and before long she will build the same thing. Their buildings, however, remain separate.

Cooperative Play

Cooperative play begins with the simple back-and-forth play of two children. They try to coordinate their actions so that they can roll a ball back and forth or take turns talking on a toy telephone. In these early interchanges, they practice with a poor the turn-taking pattern of "first me, then you." In their preschool years, they develop their interaction skills further and some group play begins to form. They learn to play together, deciding what they will play and what role they will take.

In cooperative play all the children involved take part in the same activity. They may pretend to take a trip to the library by setting up a scene with a librarian, people reading books, and a computer system to check out books. Their conversation may sound something like this:

Joe: "I'm going to be the librarian so I'll go get the books. You be the customer and come to my check-out."

Sam: "I've got all these books here. I want to take them home."

Joe: "No, you can only take a few of them, not all. Where is your library card? You got to have a card. Here, you can use this for your card."

The chart below defines the five types of social play and gives approximate age ranges for each type:

SOCIAL PLAY	
TYPE OF PLAY	**AGES THIS BEGINS**
Play with Adults Plays with parent or other adult	Birth
Solitary Play Plays alone rather than with peers	12-18 months
Parallel Play Children play side by side Activities are unrelated	2-2 1/2 years
Associative Play Children play with same materials but without creating together	2 1/2- 3 years
Cooperative Play Children create a play theme together	3-3 1/2 years

Adapted from McNellis, Ed., 1987.

SOCIODRAMATIC PLAY

When we study play we often divide play with objects from play with people. But when we observe play as it happens we see how related these two are. In dramatic play children need both the skill to manipulate and pretend with objects and the social skills used in cooperative play. We see the two types of play overlap in groups of children working together to construct a building or pretending to be child care providers. *Sociodramatic play* is the term used to describe how these two types of play come together.

Sociodramatic play is recognized as the highest level of dramatic play (Christie, 1982) because it requires the combination of social and dramatic play skills. Sara Smilansky (1968) describes six elements of play which must be present in order for play to be considered sociodramatic. The elements are listed below:

- Imitative role play
- Make-believe with objects
- Make-believe with actions and situations
- Interaction
- Verbal communication
- Persistence

Adapted from Smilansky, 1968.

Sociodramatic play prepares a child for many of life's experiences. The representational skills practiced in sociodramatic play are essential to the child's ability to conceptualize many of the things taught in school. Reading deals with symbols for language, numerical symbols represent quantities of objects, and science uses molecules to stand for the unseen. The interactions of a child in play prepares her for the give-and-take of social relationships. Creativity is strengthened as a child resolves dilemmas and expands on situations that lead to new ways to play (Smilansky, 1968, 1990).

Competent sociodramatic players have mastered the necessary skills of creativity, representation, and interaction. Many preschoolers will learn the skills needed for sociodramatic play by watching others and by playing in groups. However, not all children learn to put dramatic and social skills together in sociodramatic play through exposure to group play sessions alone. For these children, the techniques described in this book are needed to help them learn to play at this highly developed level.

CHAPTER 2

SETTING THE STAGE

Amy, Mike, and Darius are playing "fighting fires" by the climber. They have created houses with the large blocks. Amy shouts excitedly, "Oh, no! Our house is on fire!" The teacher had put out a long rubber hose and the three children are excitedly aiming the hose at the blocks. Amy says, "Oh, I think the fire is almost out." Mike yells, "Oh no, that one over there is on fire!" They quickly pull the hose to the climber. Darius leaves the group to put a block down and he beckons, "Come on, let's go in our fire truck now to the station." The climber becomes the station and the play goes on much to the enjoyment of all.

Scenes like this are witnessed over and over again in centers and homes. The play looks effortless and goes so smoothly that the caregiver may simply appreciate the children's enthusiasm and go on to more pressing tasks.

Before Amy, Mike, and Darius began playing, the caregiver did several things that contributed to the success of this play. The things done to set the stage by adults determine how *much* play children do, as well as the *quality* of the play.

In this chapter, we discuss what things adults can do to influence the quantity and quality of play. The four main factors are:

Time
Space
Props
Planned Experiences

The definitions of play in Chapter 1 emphasized the complexity of play. In the course of growing up, most children acquire play skills easily and naturally. However, adults can provide supports that increase the likelihood that children will succeed in their play together. In the example at the beginning of this chapter, the caregiver had made available equipment like the hose and climber to Amy, Mike, and Darius. She had also provided enough time so that play could develop. The adult assistance in the play is not immediately obvious to an observer. When play is going smoothly, these stage-setting tasks are the kinds of supports children need. Researchers have documented that adults can encourage high quality play in the four following ways:

- Providing an adequate amount of free-choice time
- Designing space that invites play
- Providing a large variety of props
- Providing planned experiences that are related to play

Adapted from Johnson, Christie, & Yawkey, 1987.

Brn Porter/Don Franklin

TIME

It is vital that children have enough time to plan and carry out sociodramatic play. It often takes awhile just to set up the play, choose the roles, work out conflicts, and get other children involved. It is recommended that free play periods last from thirty to fifty minutes each (Johnson, Christie, & Yawkey, 1987). If play periods are shorter than this, children may choose simpler forms of play (Johnson, Christie, & Yawkey, 1987). In our example at the beginning of the chapter, the teacher had provided a forty-five minute free play time. The exciting firefighting didn't occur until thirty minutes into that time.

SPACE

Planning an appropriate space for play is one of the biggest influences an adult can have on children's play. An environment that is well planned draws children in, but an environment that is haphazard and too open can actually increase aggression and disruption. Here are some considerations for planning a space for play:

- Arrange the room so children can see the toys and materials as they enter the room.
- Include play areas that encourage solitary, parallel, and sociodramatic play. Both block and housekeeping areas encourage more social play. Housekeeping play results in more language than other areas. Puzzles encourage more solitary play.
- Plan play experiences outdoors as well as indoors. Studies have shown that boys and children from low-income homes actually play longer and with more complexity outdoors.
- Include both a house and block area in your space.
- Create an opening between the housekeeping area and the block area so materials can be used together or moved back and forth. This can result in more boy-girl play and use of blocks as props by older children.
- Occasionally use a separate room for a play theme if possible. This heightens interest and excitement.
- When adding separate dramatic play themes to your setting—post office, fire station, or doctor's office—keep the house corner as well. Such arrangements lengthen the time children play together because children have more options to explore. As they expand their play, they use the house corner as a base for their activity.
- Set up learning centers that are well defined, enclosed, and visible. Well defined spaces increase the occurences of play more than wide open spaces. Include a variety of materials in the play areas that you set up. The following is a chart that outlines possible play areas and materials.

Johnson, Christie, & Yawkey, 1987.

PLAY AREAS	
AREAS	**MATERIALS**
Art Activities	Pencils, crayons, markers, scissors, paper, shape insets, rulers
House	Stove, refrigerator, table, dishes, play food, pots and pans, cupboards, dress-up clothes, cradle, dolls, doll clothes, telephone
Manipulative	Lego blocks, games, bristle blocks, popoids, puzzles
Blocks	Unit blocks, large blocks, cars and trucks, animals, other props for blocks
Science	Rocks, feathers, shells, fish, animals, scale, leaves, wood
Large Motor	Slide, climber, rebounder, form blocks, boxes, waffle blocks, tunnel
Sensorimotor	Sand, water, beans, cornmeal
Reading Corner	Books, puppets, record player or cassette player, flannel board

PROPS

Props are an essential part of a child's play. Any toy or material that a child uses to play is called a prop. Blocks, dress-up clothes, playdough, and Lego blocks are all props.

Caregivers need to provide a large variety of props to encourage the types of play discussed in Chapter 1 because children's play changes according to the play materials available (Johnson, Christie, & Yawkey, 1987). For instance, costumes or other theme-related props encourage more sociodramatic play than puzzles or play dough. (Children playing with puzzles or playdough often engage in solitary play.) The greater the variety of props available, the more options children will have during free choice time.

The chart below outlines the types of play and the toys or materials associated with it. With this chart, you can observe children's choices in play materials and identify which types of play individual children prefer. By expanding their choices of props, children will gain more experience in other types of play.

Types of Play Associated with Play Materials

SOCIAL PLAY	
Parallel & Solitary	**Cooperative**
Blocks Puzzles Beads Art materials Clay, playdough Sand & water Lego blocks & other manipulatives	Housekeeping toys Dolls Dress-up clothes Vehicles Blocks Lego blocks & other manipulatives

PLAY WITH OBJECTS		
Sensorimotor	**Constructive**	**Dramatic**
Bead Clay, playdough Sand & water Lego blocks	Blocks Puzzles Art materials Lego blocks	Housekeeping toys Dolls Dress-up clothes Vehicles Blocks Lego blocks

Adapted from Johnson, Christie, & Yawkey, 1987.

Besides providing many types of props, caregivers should offer a mixture of realistic and more unstructured materials. For example, a house corner could have a cradle, stove, and refrigerator, all that look real. Pretend vegetables, steak, and potatoes could be used in pots and pans. However, some unstructured materials like cardboard boxes, scraps of materials, and paper could be used for any number of play themes. Younger children, ages two, three, and four will need more real objects to maintain pretend themes. Older children, ages four, five, and six will feel comfortable incorporating cardboard boxes, featureless dolls, and blocks as well as real objects into their play. Children with cognitive, language, or behavioral delays may need real objects for a longer time to encourage pretend play. Caregivers should look at the ages and skills of the children in their care to determine how many props should be realistic.

Caregivers should provide enough props so that children are not always competing for toys. This helps reduce the number of fights and conflicts between children. There are some props that must be shared because caregivers cannot afford to buy one for each child. No day care center or home could provide a trike for every child that wants one. But some props do not involve as much expense. Caregivers can provide more of these toys.

For example, one teacher saw that the three-year-old children were constantly fighting over the plastic phones. She thought about several solutions and discussed them with her supervisor. Most of the solutions focused on teaching the children to share. The supervisor suggested buying three more phones. Once the extra phones were bought and added to the environment, the fighting over the phones stopped.

When you are deciding how many of a certain toy to include in your play space, look at the ages of the children in your group. Younger children need more of each type of the popular toys because they have less ability to share.

We have one final word about props. The props you include in your environment should reflect the cultures of the children in your care. Talk to the parents about what special things they do at home and include these activities in the children's play props. Invite parents in to share cultural interests. By doing this you encourage more play, give a sense of inclusion to all children in your setting, and teach respect for differences. Expand the children's awareness and understanding of other ethnic and racial backgrounds. Survey your environment to see if the toys and materials reflect diversity of experience, race and culture. For example, housekeeping utensils, puzzles, books, dolls, and pictures should reflect the value you place on diversity (Derman-Sparks, 1989).

PLANNED EXPERIENCES

Children may need planned experiences to successfully act out new roles in sociodramatic play. All children have some idea of roles within a household but work-related roles may be difficult for them to act out unless they have observed them. This means that adults may need to give children additional experience when introducing a new play theme. These experiences can include field trips, classroom visitations by people in different occupations, and books and video tapes about different jobs (Johnson, Christie, & Yawkey, 1987). The teacher in our first example had taken her class to the fire station the week before and the children were able to get on the truck and see much of the equipment. Later they could act out fighting a fire using props that represented this equipment.

Little did Amy, Mike, and Darius know as they became engrossed in fighting the fire that the teacher had done a great amount of behind-the-scenes work. She had set the stage for play by attending to how much time she allowed for play, how she arranged the space, what props she included in her environment, and what kinds of experiences she planned. Provide these same supports and most children will acquire the play skills they need.

After you have done this, watch the children's play. You will learn how the whole group interacts, how your space and props work, and which individual children need more help to become involved with the others.

CHAPTER 3

THE PLAY CHECKLIST

Gregory stands outside the group in the house corner and watches intently. He puckers his lips and moves closer. He watches as the other three children pretend they are a family with a mother, father, and child. The mother is setting the table and admonishing the child to drink her milk. Gregory moves closer. Then he yells and runs to grab the plate away from Marie, the mother. As she backs away, she steps on the father's toes and soon all four children are upset and calling for the adult to help them.

Many caregivers observing the scene above would be understandably upset with Gregory. He would more than likely be labeled aggressive and a behavior problem. But if we were to systematically observe him, we might find a lack of play skills underlying his aggressive behavior.

In previous chapters we have discussed general terms and techniques for use in work with groups of children. Now we begin to look at an individual having difficulty playing. In this chapter, you will find:

Guidelines for Observation
The Play Checklist
Time for Action

It is very important that you read the entire chapter before you try to use the Play Checklist. With complete information, it will be easier to accurately match the child's skill level with the checklist items.

GUIDELINES FOR OBSERVATION

To understand a child's play you must observe. By watching a child you learn:

- What she most frequently likes to play
- What toys and materials she prefers
- What areas of the room are most attractive to her
- Who her favorite playmates are
- Her play skill level

As you look at the children in your group you may notice that one child has difficulty sticking to an activity for any length of time. A second child may display some of the sociodramatic skills, like pretending with objects or playing a role, but does not interact with her peers. You may notice that a third child does not pretend with any of the materials.

In order to gain a true assessment of a child's level of play keep the following guidelines in mind:

General Observation Guidelines

1. Observe the child during a time and in a place which create an opportunity for sociodramatic play.

   In order to give the child an opportunity to demonstrate this high level of play, you must make certain that the materials she has available are conducive to role play and that there are other children around to engage in group play. Dolls, puppets, costumes, and many types of building materials promote sociodramatic play. Painting or putting puzzles together are not activities which are likely to bring about the type of play you want to observe. (For further information see Chapter 2.)

   Some children may be more comfortable pretending during outdoor play. Be sure to observe children in both indoor and outdoor play settings.

2. Make sure that the child you are observing knows the other children.

   When she is familiar with the children, a child is more likely to exhibit sociodramatic skills. Give children who are new to the setting a few weeks to adjust and get to know others before observing them.

3. Observe a child two or three times in order to get a true picture of the child's skill level.

   If you obtain only one sampling of the child's skills, you may watch the child on a day she isn't feeling well or on a day that her usual playmates are unavailable. This could greatly influence the results that you get.

Use the running record method when you observe. To observe in this way, separate yourself from the group, explaining to the children that you are going to watch them play for a while. Write down everything that is taking place. You may need to develop a shorthand of sorts or codes for certain names and words in order to keep up with the action.

Be careful to write down only the things that are observable to all onlookers. This method will keep your comments from becoming judgmental. Record what you see using objective terms and avoiding subjective statements. For example, to say "Sally is unhappy" makes a subjective judgment about Sally's feelings. To say "Sally's head was down. She made no eye contact. She frowned," is objective. Anyone looking at Sally at the same time would record her behavior in a similar manner because the statements are based on observable facts.

A running record of a play scenario in which we focused on Sally might read something like this:

Four children at the water table, washing dolls.

Sally leans over table.
Pushes doll's stomach.
Gavin: "Sally watch."
Sally glances briefly.
Sally: "Her taking a bath."
Kari pulls at Sally's arm.
No response.
Kari: "Move it Sally!"
No response.
Sally twirls doll on head.
Picks up doll, looks at doll's face.
Smooths doll's hair.

Michael Siluk

Sally: "I need a towel."
Teacher: "I hear you Sally."
Sally: "I need a towel."
Sally: "I need a towel."

From the example you can see that correct grammar and complete sentence structure are not necessary. In fact, you would probably abbreviate further and find a way to identify the children without writing out their names each time. The important thing to remember is to record accurate information, written in a way that enables you to describe the situation to others or to recreate it in your own mind's eye.

The information you record in the observations will be used as the basis for completing the Play Checklist.

THE PLAY CHECKLIST

The Play Checklist has been developed to help adults observe and understand a child's sociodramatic play skills. This checklist consists of ten sections. The first five are an adaptation of Smilansky's Play Inventory (1968) (Christie, 1982). The second five take a closer look at social skills that are needed to succeed in sociodramatic play.

The categories included in the checklist are:

Pretending with Objects
Role-playing
Verbalizations about the Play Scenario
Verbal Communication During a Play Episode
Persistence in Play
Interactions
Entrance to a Play Group
Conflict Management
Turn-taking
Support of Peers

This is a tool that you can use with each child in your group, but it was designed to be used with the child who is having difficulty with play. You might be able to quickly pick out the child who needs to be observed. If you need help in deciding, the following guidelines will assist you:

- The child consistently has trouble with a small group of children or with one particular child.
- The child is always choosing to play alone and never joins a group in play.
- The child doesn't role-play by age five.
- The child does not talk during play by age four and a half.
- The child refuses to take turns.

- The child does not pretend with imaginary objects by four and a half.

If you see these behaviors or are just troubled by a child's lack of interest in play, use the checklist to get a fuller picture of the child's skills and where you can help.

There are many reasons why children do not join in group play. Lack of group experience, temperament, home environment, or developmental delays can all affect a child's play skills. You cannot change factors such as temperament or home environment, but you can help a child use the play experience to learn and grow if you understand where the child can use extra help. The checklist can give you a place to start.

Instructions

To use the Play Checklist, decide which child you will observe during free play. Focus on this child and do two or three running records of about ten to fifteen minutes in length. It would be most helpful if you observe an entire play scene, even if it runs longer than fifteen minutes, but this may not be possible given the needs of your group of children.

After completing the running records, check the highest skill on the Play Checklist that you see the child perform. The individual items under each section heading have been ordered from the easiest skill to the most complex. You may find that the child is capable of one of the higher level skills on occasion, but seems to use a lower level play skill more consistently. If this is the case, check the one the child uses most often.

PLAY CHECKLIST

Date: ____________________

Name: ____________________

Date of Birth: ____________________

Check the highest level skills you consistently observe:

*1. Pretending with Objects
- ❑ Does not use objects to pretend
- ❑ Uses real objects
- ❑ Substitutes objects for other objects
- ❑ Uses imaginary objects

*2. Role-Playing
- ❑ No role play
- ❑ Uses one sequence of play
- ❑ Combines sequences
- ❑ Uses verbal declaration (i.e., "I'm a doctor.")
- ❑ Imitates actions of role, including dress

*3. Verbalizations about Play Scenario
- ❑ Does not use pretend words during play
- ❑ Uses words to describe substitute objects
- ❑ Uses words to describe imaginary objects and actions (i.e., "I'm painting a house.")
- ❑ Uses words to create a play scenario (i.e., "Let's say we're being taken by a monster.")

*4. Verbal Communication during a Play Episode
- ❑ Does not verbally communicate during play
- ❑ Talks during play only to self
- ❑ Talks only to adults in play
- ❑ Talks with peers in play by stepping outside of role
- ❑ Talks with peers from within role (i.e., "Eat your dinner before your dad comes home.")

*5. Persistence in Play
- ❑ Less than five minutes
- ❑ Six to nine minutes
- ❑ Ten minutes or longer

6. Interactions
- ❑ Plays alone
- ❑ Plays only with adults
- ❑ Plays with one child, always the same person
- ❑ Plays with one child, can be different partners
- ❑ Can play with two or three children all together

#7. Entrance to a Play Group
- ❑ Does not attempt to enter play group
- ❑ Uses force to enter play group
- ❑ Stands near group and watches
- ❑ Imitates behavior of group
- ❑ Makes comments related to play theme
- ❑ Gets attention of another child before commenting

8. Conflict Management
- ❑ Gives in during conflict
- ❑ Uses force to solve conflicts
- ❑ Seeks adult assistance
- ❑ Imitates verbal solutions provided by adults
- ❑ Recalls words to use when reminded
- ❑ Initiates use of words
- ❑ Accepts reasonable compromises

9. Turn-Taking
- ❑ Refuses to take turns
- ❑ Leaves toys: protests when others pick them up
- ❑ Gives up toy easily if done with it
- ❑ Gives up toy if another child asks for it
- ❑ Takes turns if arranged and directed by an adult
- ❑ Asks for turn, does not wait for a response
- ❑ Proposes turn taking; will take and give turns

10. Support of Peers
- ❑ Shows no interest in peers
- ❑ Directs attention to distress of peers
- ❑ Offers help
- ❑ Offers and takes suggestions of peers at times
- ❑ Encourages or praises peers

Note: The developmental progression outlined in each segment of the play checklist can be used as a guideline when assessing most children's development. However, not all individuals will go through the same steps in development nor through the same developmental sequence.

Sections marked with * are adapted from: Smilansky, S. 1968. *The Effects of Sociodramatic Play on Disadvantaged Preschool Children.* New York: Wiley

Sections marked with # are adapted from: Hazen, Black, & Fleming-Johnson. "Social Acceptance." *Young Children* 39 (1984): 26-36.

From *Pathways to Play: Developing Play Skills in Young Children.* Redleaf Press, 450 N. Syndicate, St. Paul, MN 55104, 1-800-423-8309.

Explanation of the Play Checklist

The following is a detailed explanation of each of the individual sections of the Play Checklist.

1. Pretending with Objects

This is one of the first skills a child acquires in play. At around twelve to eighteen months, a child begins to use objects in a dramatically new way. Instead of just exploring their physical properties, the child begins to pretend with them. The child not only picks up and puts down the telephone, she *talks* when the receiver is near her mouth. Now she is beginning to symbolize. The smooth transition between these two stages underplays the truly dramatic and exciting beginnings of pretending.

It may be difficult to always interpret accurately how a child is using an object. As you cannot see inside the child's mind, you need to observe her behaviors and listen to her language. Most of the time, if you understand the child's frame of reference, you will be able to see how she is pretending with objects.

- Does not use objects to pretend

  This means that the child simply uses objects to bang, roll, drop, or push. All the action is done to explore physical properties, *not* to pretend.

- Uses real objects

  By eighteen months most children begin to use real objects or child-sized replicas to pretend. For example, a child may use a bottle to feed a doll or may pretend to cook by stirring with a spoon in a pan. At this level, the child almost always needs an object that looks like the real thing to pretend. If given substitutes, the child may ignore them.

- Substitutes objects for other objects

  A child can increasingly use more dissimilar objects to pretend. For instance, a child may use a block as a bed for the baby and a few months later use a blanket or rug as a bed. A child who cannot do this will seek out a more realistic prop to use.

- Uses imaginary objects

  By age four most children no longer need an object to pretend. They use action and words to indicate imaginary objects. In our experience many children do this first with imaginary food or imaginary money. Gradually, the child learns that even if she doesn't have an object, the play doesn't have to stop. She can *pretend* to have the object.

2. Role-Playing

This section highlights a child's ability to act out a role in play. Certainly, most children find role-playing to be delightful. They quickly don the fire-fighter hats and coats to fight the fire. This requires a complex understanding of *how* the role is played. Children use voice, dress, body language, and props to communicate that understanding.

- No role-play

  The child uses no props, language, or actions to play a role. She may lack the cognitive understanding of what a role is or may be afraid to risk role-play in a group.

- Uses one sequence of play

  In early role-playing, toddlers pretend just one incident. For example, a two-year old may pick up the telephone, say hello, and hang up. Or she may put a bottle to a doll's mouth for a few seconds and then throw the bottle and the doll aside.

- Combines sequences

  As a child matures, she learns to combine play events so they become more complex. For example, Monica stirs a spoon in a pan at the stove in the house corner and then sets the table. Combining these distinct and separate events into one continuous flow builds up to playing a role in an elaborate and unique style.

- Uses verbal declaration (i.e., "I'm the doctor.")

  A child may verbally indicate he is the dad or a firefighter. However, this may or may not be supported by dress, actions, and language appropriate to that role. If the child does not elaborate beyond the verbal declaration, the child may need help to further play out the role. For example, Ali would run into the doctor play and say, "I'm the doctor." He would then run out. His caregiver helped him do the actions of a doctor by encouraging him to put on the white coat, take a blood pressure reading, and give a shot.

- Imitates actions of role, including dress

  The child has the ability to imitate roles in play such as doctor, parent, super hero, or baby. She will use dress, actions or body language, props, voice, and words to play out her understanding of what others in that role *do*. The child learns what each role requires by watching adults, watching television or movies, and reading books. Unless a child can succeed in role-playing, she will have real difficulty with sociodramatic play in a group. She will be quickly left behind in the ongoing action.

3. Verbalizations about Play Scenario

Children use language during play to let their play partners know where the play is going. Without words, children lose track of the collective play theme and play disintegrates. In this section of the checklist, we look at the child's words that build the pretend theme.

These words may or may not be spoken to others in play.

- Does not use pretend words during play

  If you check this item for a child the child probably is not talking much during play. A child with a language delay or a shy temperament would have difficulty with verbalizations.

- Uses words to describe substitute objects

  The child will use words to communicate to other children or adults what a substitute object represents. For instance, a child may put a piece of paper in another child's hand and state, "Here's a rock for the wall."

- Uses words to describe imaginary objects and actions

  The child will use words to communicate what an object or action is. For instance, a child may be standing in front of the wall and moving her arm up and down the wall, saying, "I'm painting now."

- Uses words to create a play scenario

  This last item is the most difficult skill. The child uses words to create a scene. You may see a child outline a scene which a group of children will then enter. For example, Sarah said loudly, "Let's say this is an ocean and we are on this boat and there's a whole bunch of sharks after us." If the group of children agrees to this scene, the play begins.

4. Verbal Communication during a Play Episode

Not only do children use words to create agreement on actions and themes, they use language to direct others or communicate with others during play. Unless this verbal interaction occurs, children play their roles alone with little communication between them. Gestural language such as sign language can perform the same function. Language or gestural communication becomes the "glue" that holds the play together.

- Does not use words during play

  The child does not speak during play episodes. Sometimes this child is an onlooker. Other times she will be in the middle of a play group, but will attempt no verbal communication.

- Talks during play, only to self

  The child may talk but the words aren't directed or intended as communication. The child may simply be talking to herself. This is used by many children to further their individual play, but it doesn't help the child integrate into the group play.

- Talks only with adults in play

  The child talks with an adult to ask for toys or materials or to describe what she is doing. She may ask for help with sensorimotor tasks like buttoning the buttons on a doll's shirt.

- Talks with peers in play by stepping outside of role

  The child will direct comments to others, but steps out of a role temporarily to do it. When a child does this she may tell another child how to play a role or correct the other child's actions. For example, Mary stops feeding the baby long enough to tell John, "No John! That's not where the daddy sits."

- Talks with peers from within role

  The most sophisticated way to verbally communicate during play is to talk from inside of the role. A skilled child will be able to give suggestions or direct others in their respective roles by playing the mom or teacher or doctor. In the example above, if Mary had learned this skill, she could say in her mommy voice, "No dear, you sit over here." When this skill is achieved, there are fewer breaks in the play.

5. Persistence in Play

This section examines how long a child may play *in a group* as part of a sociodramatic play theme. A child with a short attention span will have difficulty staying in one place, much less playing with a group. A child may also play alone longer than with a group, but use this section to measure time in a group play episode.

This will be an important skill to observe more than one time. Even children who are typically capable of persisting may be interrupted easily if they are playing in high traffic areas with many distractions.

- Less than five minutes

  Toddlers flit from activity to activity, but most three year olds should be able to join in group play for as long as four minutes.

- Six to nine minutes

  Four year olds should increasingly expand their group play times to nine minutes.

- Ten minutes or longer

  Most five year olds can sustain a sociodramatic play episode with other children for ten minutes or longer.

6. Interactions

In sociodramatic play a child will interact with at least one other child. They exchange ideas, conversation, and materials as they work together to create playful scenes.

- Plays alone

  The child who plays alone is sometimes thought of as a loner or withdrawn child. She tends to be on the outskirts of the group's activities and may isolate herself further by choosing activities and materials that are typically used by one person at a time, such as easel painting or working with beads.

- Plays only with adults

  Adults can become a child's primary play partners if the child is uncomfortable with her peers. She can be quite demanding of adult attention and unsure of what to do with herself when the adult is unavailable to her. The child might look to the adult to provide play ideas and to keep play going. For example, Michael preferred to be with one caregiver and followed her around the classroom. When she was unavailable, Michael was at a loss for appropriate play ideas and went to the water table to play alone.

- Plays with one other child, always the same person

  People consider this child to have only one "best friend." She has learned to get along adequately with this best friend but seems unable to transfer the interaction skills to play with any other children.

- Plays with one child, can be different partners

  A child interacting at this level will play with a number of different children but she needs to play one-on-one. Her partners may switch from day to day or from activity to activity. At this point she is still unable to play in groups of three so she may reject others.

- Can play with two or three children all together

  Playing with two or three others in a group is the most sophisticated level of interaction. The child who knows how to do this pays attention to the other children and is capable of some give and take.

Francis Wardle

7. Entrance to a Play Group (Adapted from Hazen, Black, & Fleming-Johnson, 1984.)

This skill differs from the interaction skills discussed above in a subtle way. It refers to the child's ability to enter into a group of children that have already established a play scenario.

- Does not attempt to enter play group

  A child who does not attempt to enter a play group may be somewhat disconnected from the others. She may not attend to other's behavior or their verbalizations. This child plays alone frequently and may decline the play invitations of other children.

- Uses force to enter play group

  Many types of force may be mistakenly tried to enter the play of others. Children may initiate contacts with others by patting them on the back, poking their arm, wrestling them to the ground, or using verbal threats such as, "I'm not going to be your friend anymore." These attempts to make contact are rarely successful.

- Stands near group and watches

  Sometimes standing near the group and watching the established play can be an effective method of gaining entry. The child becomes enveloped as the play of the group surrounds her.

- Imitates behavior of group

  As above, the child stands near the group but this time begins to perform the same type of activities. The child is usually on the outskirts of the group but instead of just watching she imitates their behaviors. Once again the play of the group surrounds her.

- Makes comments related to play theme

  Using this strategy to enter play, the child comes into the group and says something related to what the other children are doing. When Marie came up to a group of children playing school she said, "How about we go on a field trip to the zoo?"

- Gets attention of another child before commenting

  The most effective strategy a child can use is to call a child's name, establish eye contact, or tap her shoulder to get her attention before making a comment that is related to the existing play. Building on the example above, Marie would have said, "Josh, how about if we go on a field trip to the zoo?"

8. Conflict Management

For many preschoolers conflicts occur because they don't agree about who should play with a toy or what they should play. If problems cannot be resolved in a way that is acceptable to all those involved, play will fall apart or individuals will be left out.

- Gives in during conflict

  Some children respond to conflict in a passive manner. A child who gives in will leave the area or go on to another activity when someone takes her toy. Sometimes this child looks very surprised that another person would take her toy and may look as if she doesn't know what to do in a conflict situation. Others choose not to respond.

- Uses force to solve conflicts

  Preschoolers often try to solve problems through the use of force. Force can mean physical aggression, verbal aggression, manipulation, or physical intimidation. Preschoolers with poor language skills are more likely to try to get a toy by using aggression because of the difficulty they have in making themselves understood. Others may verbally threaten their peers by saying, "I'm going to let you have it if you don't give me the Big Wheel." A child may even try to bully someone by standing over him and puffing out his chest while showing his clenched fist.

- Seeks adult assistance

  When a child has little problem-solving ability she relies on the adult to solve it for her. She might start crying when she has a problem and looks toward the adult, or she might come to the adult to complain about a situation that she doesn't know how to handle. Most often the adult must go with the child to assist her in solving the problem.

- Imitates verbal solutions provided by the adult

  While the child may not be able to solve the conflict by herself, she can use the words that the adult gives her. The adult must provide the child with the appropriate words to use in the situation. The child is responsible for going back to the conflict situation and imitating the words given.

- Recalls words to use when reminded

  A child at this level still goes to the adult for help when faced with a problem. The adult reminds her of how to solve the problem by giving a direction such as, "Use your words." She is then able to go back to the situation and use some of the words she recalls having learned in the past.

- Initiates use of words

  After much practice a child learns to use words to solve conflicts on her own. She needs no reminders or help in thinking of the words to use. But she may need help in getting the other child to listen to her or to follow through with her request.

- Accepts reasonable compromises

  Children who are able to accept reasonable compromises in problem-solving situations know how to use words to get their needs met and can sometimes do as another child asks.

9. Turn-Taking

In group child care settings we ask children to learn to share at a very early age. Because of a limited number of resources, children must learn to take turns with toys, equipment, and adult attention. In order to successfully take turns, a child must understand give-and-take. She must learn to temporarily delay her own satisfaction in order to coordinate her behavior with others. In addition, she must know how to negotiate a trade or a deal and sometimes accept the suggestions made by others. This is closely related to the child's ability to manage conflict.

- Refuses to take turns

  It is not uncommon for a child to refuse to take turns. If she is forced to share a possession she may prefer to leave the area rather than share something that she is not ready to give up. A young child may have a tantrum when asked to share an item. An older child may say, "I'm not playing if I can't have the one I want."

- Leaves toys; protests when others pick them up

  A child will leave a toy that she has been playing with but will still feel that it is hers. She may become upset and demand back a toy that someone else has picked up. D.J. had been using the yellow truck in the sand but left the area to greet another child who had just arrived. When D.J. returned he found Jeremy had picked up the yellow truck and was driving it around. He yelled, "Hey, I was using that."

- Gives up toy easily if done with it

  As a child matures, she will leave a toy she is finished with. She understands that toys she leaves might not be in the exact same place when she returns and that others may use them.

- Give up toy if another child asks for it

  A child will share a material when she is asked only when she feels done with it. A typical response would be, "That's okay, I'm done anyway," or "Sure, I'm going to play with the dump truck now."

- Takes turns if arranged and directed by an adult

  Some children need an adult to structure turn-taking. For instance, the adult may tell the child how to judge when the other is done, set limits on the number of children using a material, or divide up toys among the players. Whatever type of adult intervention is used, a child at this level will be able to agree to the turn-taking propositions.

- Asks for turn, does not wait for a response

  When a child begins to learn to ask for a turn she uses the words to ask but sometimes leaves out the pause that gives the other person a chance to respond. The child does not understand that she needs to wait for the other person and so the words and the taking of the item take place simultaneously. For instance, when Jackie asked for a towel she said, "Can I have a towel, Ellie?" At the same time she took it from Ellie's hand.

- Proposes turn-taking; will take and give turns

  Play can proceed smoothly when a child has successfully learned to share a piece of equipment. Learning to share means being able to both give and take turns.

10. Support of Peers

Being able to support your peers is important to starting and maintaining friendships. This is difficult for many younger children, who may be at a very egocentric stage in their development. It requires that a child learn to look at a situation from another person's position, empathize with other's feelings, offer comfort or help, establish a balance in giving and taking suggestions that help play to continue, and develop positive attitudes toward others (Asher, Renshaw, & Hymel, 1982).

- Shows no interest in peers

  To stand and watch others seems simple enough, yet some children do not notice the actions and expressions of others. An impulsive, active, or self-absorbed child may have difficulty showing interest in her peers.

- Directs attention to distress of peers

  A young child will pay attention to others in the room who are crying or upset. She stops what she is doing momentarily and looks in the direction of the other child. She may even move closer to the child who is upset.

- Offers help

  Not only does this child pay attention to another child in the room who is crying or upset; she will also try to help. She will hold out a cuddly, stuffed animal or a blanket to provide comfort. She may try to hug or pat the back of a child who is upset. Her actions suggest that she understands how the other child feels and wants to help her feel better.

- Offers and takes suggestions of peers at times

  When two or three children are playing together they must share in the planning and leadership roles of play. A child capable of this will go along with the suggestions of others and may say something like, "Yeah, let's do that," or "That's a good idea." At other times, the child will offer play ideas, saying, "Let's pretend...," or "How about if we..." There should be some balance in suggesting scenes to play and accepting those of others.

- Encourages or praises peers

  This child is able to recognize the strengths of other children and comment on them or to notice and say something about a child who is working hard or doing a good job. For instance, as Marcia arrived at child care Lexi said, "That's a neat sweatshirt, Marcia."

TIME FOR ACTION

Now that we have discussed observing a child and filling out the checklist it is time for you to try these techniques. Pick out a child in your care that you are concerned about. Refer to the guidelines presented in this chapter to decide if you want to do a checklist. If so, do two to three running records during free play. With the more detailed information about the child you can complete a checklist. After you have done this, you will have a clearer understanding of the child and her skills.

> Remember to do the checklist from two to three observations, rather than during a direct observation. You need the information from several different observations to complete the picture of a child. Be sure the observations are in varied settings, with opportunities for a variety of play for the child. For more on observations, see page 20.

CHAPTER 4

PLANNING FROM THE PLAY CHECKLIST

Asheley is a four year old who rarely engages in sociodramatic play. She chooses most often to paint at the easel or to play in the water table. From time to time her caregiver finds her in the housekeeping area. She plays with the same doll each time she plays there. When no one else is using the doll, she finds it and pretends to feed or dress it. She doesn't say much while playing. Asheley's play is short-lived and does not involve much pretend play.

When her caregiver did a Play Checklist for Asheley she found Asheley was having difficulty interacting with others, role-playing, and using language during play. In this chapter we will look at how to use the information from the Play Checklist to plan for a child like her and those you observed. The chapter will include:

Understanding the Information
Writing Goals
Developing Teaching Strategies
Time for Action

UNDERSTANDING THE INFORMATION

Once you have completed a checklist you will need to know how to interpret and use the information. As we said before, the Play Checklist is not intended to assess developmental lags but rather to help plan for children who have difficulty playing (see Chapter 3). When you use it you will notice that there are no age ratings on the Play Checklist to indicate when a child should be performing a particular skill. However, young preschoolers, ages two and a half to three, would be expected to demonstrate the skills and behaviors at the lower end of each section and older preschoolers, ages four and a half to five could be expected to be developing the more sophisticated skills at the upper end.

When you marked the highest level skills the child is consistently performing on the Play Checklist, you established the child's *current level of functioning*. In some cases, you will discover that a child's current level of functioning seems to be at an appropriate level. That child may only need your continued encouragement to learn further play skills.

However, other children in your group may be having difficulty performing even the most basic skills. These children may not be gaining play skills in the ways other children do. Asheley, in our example at the beginning of this chapter, is one of these children. Although Asheley is four years old, she is demonstrating skills at the lower end of the sequences. The Role-playing section of her Play Checklist is presented below to illustrate her current level of functioning in this area.

1. Role-Playing
   - ☐ No role-play
   - ☒ Uses one sequence of play
   - ☐ Combines sequences
   - ☐ Uses verbal declaration (i.e., "I'm a doctor.")
   - ☐ Imitates actions of role, including dress

Asheley is likely to need additional, well-planned play experiences to further the development of her role-playing and other play skills.

After you have completed checklists on children in your group, you must choose which children will benefit from a plan to improve their play skills. Here are general guidelines to use when you are making this decision:

- The child demonstrates low play skills on two to three sections on the Play Checklist.
- The child demonstrates a very low skill on one of the sections of the Play Checklist. For example, the child does not pretend with objects by age three.
- The child shows anxiety when others are playing and he is not included.
- The child often becomes aggressive when children are playing together in a group.
- The child remains a withdrawn onlooker for longer than six months.

WRITING GOALS

Once you have decided that a child will benefit from planned play experiences, begin planning by writing a few clear, concise goals.

In order to write goals, you need to decide on which area or areas to focus. Use the child's current level of functioning and the information from your observations to support your decision. If the child has a number of areas in which he needs to improve, you may have a difficult job prioritizing which skills to work on first. This may be a little like the difficulty in determining if the chicken or the egg came first. In some cases you will have to decide if the child needs to improve language skills in order to interact with others or to increase interaction skills as a way to improve language. You will want to work on the areas of greatest concern first. After a few weeks of practice, if adequate progress is not being made in the area you have chosen, you may want to change your focus to see if you can make more progress in another area.

Goals must take the child from where he is currently functioning in a skill and help him to move to the next level of difficulty. The Play Checklist has been written so that the sections move in this type of progression. That is, once you have marked the current level of functioning in a section, *the goal is the next skill listed* in the sequence. Because children develop at their own individual rates you may find exceptions to the progressions that have been outlined but it is our belief that in the majority of cases the progression of the items will be of help as you develop goals.

When you write goals answer three questions:

- Who?
- Does what?
- How well or how often?

If we were to write a goal for Asheley we would note that her current level of functioning is "Uses one sequence of play." The next level of difficulty on the Play Checklist is "Combines sequences." This becomes the root of the goal. For example, our goal for Asheley might be:

Asheley combines two sequences of play during two out of three free play periods.

Each of the three questions is answered in this goal:

• Who?	Asheley
• Does what?	combines two sequences of play
• How well or how often?	during two out of three free play periods.

Writing goals in this way helps to focus on skill development. In addition, the goal is written so that it is easy to determine if it has been met. In the beginning, develop only one or two goals for a child. Keep the goals simple enough so that they are achievable. This allows both you and the child to experience success. If you try to move a child to a new skill too soon, the child is unlikely to respond to your efforts. Review the level of difficulty you expect from the child. If you have not made too big a jump in skills, be persistent in your teaching and creative in your approaches. Give the child time.

Set a target completion date or a re-evaluation date so that you commit to working on the goal for a period of three to four months. When the target date arrives (or if progress is made sooner), observe again to see if the child is performing the desired behavior and compare your new observations to the written goal. If the goal has been reached it is time to start the process over by completing a new Play Checklist, writing new goals, and developing additional teaching strategies.

DEVELOPING TEACHING STRATEGIES

You will need to think about a number of things as you develop your strategies for teaching the new skill to the child. The following list of five questions will assist you as you begin to make plans to work with a child. Your answers to these questions should include thoughtful consideration of the child's overall skill level and interests.

1. When will you work on the goal?

   Will work take place spontaneously during play or at group times? Does the child need to work on this during a time when he can work with you on an individual basis? Should you work with him during free play? Would the child enjoy more active play or quiet activities? Is this something that can be addressed in a large group activity? Will you try to pair this child with another who can help him?

2. What are the child's special interests?

   What activities does the child most enjoy? Is that the activity you should use in your work with him? Do you want to start with an activity in which the child has had many successes and then slowly introduce a new play idea or theme? Is there an activity from his culture or family life that would be appropriate with which to start?

3. How many children will be involved?

   Does this child need one-on-one attention? Is the child doing well playing with one other child in particular? Should a third child be introduced to the play group? Can you work on the skill with a small group?

Can the size of the group vary as children come and go in a play space? If you work with a child individually, what will the other children be doing? Will others be with another adult; will they do the same activity while you sit next to and focus on the child having difficulty; or will you arrange for an additional adult to come in to work with the others as you and the child work in another room?

4. Where will the play take place?

   Will you be in your usual setting or will you arrange a special space for the activity? Will you take the child to quiet space away from the traffic of other children? Does the child engage in more sociodramatic play outside? Would outside be the best place for the activity?

5. What props will be needed?

   Is the child still using real objects in his play? What similar materials might be substituted for those real objects? Is the child ready for more abstract materials that can represent the real item? What props are essential for the play to take place? What materials would enhance the play? What additional materials might the child request?

You may recognize this stage as beginning the "lesson planning" that is done before teaching any group or activity. All of the things mentioned are important to the success of the strategy.

Bm Porter/Don Franklin

TIME FOR ACTION

Use the information you have gained through the Play Checklist and your observations to write one or two goals for the child you have chosen. Phrases from the checklist can be used as the core of your goals. Writing a goal is only a first step, and from here you can develop a number of lesson plans. In these plans you will address when a lesson will happen, where it will take place, and what materials will be used. In the next chapter we continue to help you design your plan by discussing your role during play and providing a planning form for your use.

CHAPTER 5

PLANNING YOUR ROLE

Jerome is sitting on the couch. He has a steering wheel propped on his lap as he pretends to take a journey in the child care van. Suddenly Jerome roars "Vrooooom! Vrooooom! We're stuck in the snow." Gloria, Jerome's caregiver, offers to push. She wants to help Jerome learn to interact with others. To draw additional players in, she asks other children in the area to help too. They put their shoulders to the bench, grunting and pushing, and the bench inches forward. Gloria says, "There, how's that?" Jerome answers, "Not fine yet." So Gloria and the children push again. Finally Jerome yells, "We're out!" The children climb onto the bench and join Jerome in his adventure.

One of the most important parts of your plan to help an individual child succeed in play is deciding what your role will be in the play. Most preschoolers no longer need an adult to be present in play as a partner. They need someone to provide time, space, props, and experiences. They need a resource person to help them solve conflicts. The resource person helps the children to sustain, modify, and extend the play (Chafel & Childers, 1986). However, the child with limited play skills may need not just a resource person, but an adult to play with her to move her into higher levels of play skills.

When Gloria decided to join Jerome's play she moved from a resouce person to a play partner. She took on a role by pushing the van from the snow, and she encouraged group interaction when she invited other children to join the play. However, the pacing of the play and the story line remained Jerome's, as he decided they were not out of the snow yet.

To understand why this child needs an adult as a play partner, let's review how a baby learns to play. The first play partner a baby has is her parent. Peek-a-boo, So Big, and rough-housing are all ways the baby plays with the adult. The toddler learns to "play house" from watching her parents cook, clean, and care for her. Then as a preschooler, the child branches out to include other children in the play. For varied reasons, the child with limited play skills does not easily include other children in her play. To help the child take this step, the adult must become the all-important play partner, much as the parent does for a baby.

In the previous chapter, we outlined a way to plan to teach play skills. Now we will explore roles you can take in play, how to decide on a role, and case studies as examples of planning for play. In this chapter, we discuss the following:

Roles You Can Take In Play
Which Role to Use
The Case Studies
Time for Action

ROLES YOU CAN TAKE IN PLAY

Wood, McMahon, and Cranstoun (1980) found that parallel play, co-playing, and play tutoring are three ways teachers interact when playing with children. Each of these categories produces different effects on children's play.

As we describe these kinds of involvement, you may recognize them. You probably have played with children in these ways in the past. Now you will use your role in play as a way to help a child overcome specific play difficulties.

Parallel Playing

When parallel playing, the adult plays next to the child or makes suggestions about the play. For instance, a caregiver will play next to a child by the sandbox. She will put sand in containers and dump them out while the child is building roads. The teacher may make comments about what she is doing but not about what the child is doing.

Parallel playing can be helpful in a number of situations. It is particularly helpful for a withdrawn child who becomes more withdrawn when an adult gives direct attention. This way of involving yourself in the play can also help children play longer. You can show the child that her play is important and that you value play. The child may also learn new ways to use materials (Wood,

McMahon, & Cranstoun, 1980). However, parallel play will not teach the child new sociodramatic play skills.

Co-playing

In co-playing the adult joins play that is already started and lets the children control the play. The adult influences the play by asking for instructions, and responding to the children's actions and comments. The adult does not direct the play, but offers contributions. The children can always reject any new direction to the play that the adult suggests.

Here is an example of a teacher co-playing with children in the house area.

> The teacher is watching Mary, David, and Allie play together as a family. Mary is the mother, David the father, and Allie is the child. They are eating supper together, but aren't talking very much. The teacher knocks on the cupboard and asks, "Can I come in?" David jumps up and says, "Sure." The teacher says, "I just want to come and see you. I'm your neighbor." David grabs a chair and says, "You can sit down here." Mary laughs and says "Here, you want some supper?" She hands the teacher a plate and explains, "This is spaghetti." The teacher pretends to eat it and says, "This is wonderful. I was really hungry." The teacher sits for a few seconds eating and then exclaims, "I'm thirsty. Do you have coffee?" Mary answers, "No, no coffee today." The teacher says, "Okay. What did you do today at work?" All three children jump in with descriptions of their day at work.

The teacher influences the play and enriches it by adding a new element, eating spaghetti. She also asks about work to begin more conversation. There is more language and more interest in the play when she takes part in it. When the children do not want coffee as part of the play, she graciously goes in another direction, rather than insist on the coffee.

Co-playing, like parallel playing, helps children play longer and gives children the sense that play is important. The teacher can expand the play in a nondirective way. Sometimes new children can be brought into the play (e.g. as the neighbor's children). However, the children do not learn new play skills. Therefore this strategy works best when children already have a fairly high level of play, but are bogged down or stuck in one play theme. Children who only play alone or who don't pretend will never give the adult an opportunity to join their pretend play because there is no ongoing play scene (Johnson, Christie, & Yawkey, 1987).

Sometimes co-playing can be an excellent way to help children maintain skills they have learned through play tutoring (Johnson, Christie, & Yawkey, 1987).

Play Tutoring

Play tutoring is an important role for an adult caring for children. Although it resembles co-playing, it differs in three crucial ways:

- the adult often begins the play scene rather than joining one already started by the children
- the adult assumes at least partial control over the play
- the adult teaches new play behaviors within that episode

Johnson, Christie, & Yawkey, 1987.

Two types of play tutoring were used by Smilansky (1968) to teach children play behaviors: inside the play and outside the play.

Outside the Play

When an adult uses play tutoring from outside the play she does not join the play but sits close by, making comments and suggestions to the children. These comments and suggestions guide the play and help the children learn the skills the adult plans to teach. For example, the caregiver has been watching Johnny for a few weeks as he plays. He consistently stays outside the play of the group. He builds large buildings with the blocks, but will leave the structures immediately if another child joins him. The caregiver decides to use play tutoring from the outside to help Johnny interact with one to two other children. She sets up the large blocks by the house corner and tells Johnny, "The family in this house wants to build another room onto their house. Can you start it?" Two other children approach the house corner. The caregiver invites them to be the family. They enthusiastically enter the play. The caregiver protects Johnny's role by suggesting roles and activities for them. As Johnny builds the room the caregiver sits close by and makes comments about the building. Later, as Johnny finishes his room, she suggests that he ask the family to come into the room. He waves his hand toward them and the family enters the new room with delight. Although it may take a long time for Johnny to truly interact in a sociodramatic play scene, repeated short exposures like this with an adult's support will help Johnny increasingly enjoy play with others.

In the example above the caregiver used questions, comments, and suggestions to help the child in his play. Following is a chart of the kinds of remarks that can be made to address the child's goal:

Comments	You're setting the table for four people. (Interactions)
	You have a nice couch. (Pretending with objects)
Suggestions	If you put in a door your friends can visit. (Interactions)
	Here's a bed, try this. (Pretending with objects)
Questions	Are you the mom or the child? (Role-playing)
	Are you in the ocean or the boat? (Verbalizations about the scenario)

Inside the Play

The other type of play tutoring is from inside the play. The adult takes on a role in the play and becomes an active participant. The adult, from that vantage point, can model many of the behaviors she wishes to teach.

For instance, in the previous example, the teacher used play tutoring from the outside. However, if she had become another workman with Johnny or a member of the family, she would have influenced the play from the inside. From those roles, she could have introduced new pretend elements, such as hammer and nails. Or she could have engaged the family members to help design or decorate the room. This powerful adult model can often help children gain new play skills quickly.

Both types of play tutoring can be extremely helpful to children. However, there is one strong caution. Both types can be very intrusive in children's play. Play tutoring from the inside is, of course, more intrusive than from the outside. Too much adult participation can actually hinder the spontaneity and enthusiasm that is so central to group play development.

Because of the danger of too much adult input, it is important that you move back to a co-playing or an observer role after play behaviors have been learned. That withdrawal should be gradual. For instance, if you have been playing with the children to increase their language in play, you may want to sit next to where the play is taking place as the next step and make comments to keep the play going.

WHICH ROLE TO USE

Deciding which role to use as you play with children should be based on the child's needs. To help with this Wolfgang, Mackender, and Wolfgang (1981) describe a Teacher Behavior Continuum. They suggest that the more difficulty the child has playing, the more involved the caregiver must be. As the child gains more control or skill the adult can move to less involvement. Following is an example of the continuum:

Level of Caregiver Participation				
More				Less
Physical Involvement	Directive Statements	Questions	Nondirective Statements	Visually Looking on and Reinforcing

Adapted from Wolfgang, Mackender, & Wolfgang, 1981.

This model can also be applied to the adult roles we have discussed. Play tutoring from inside the play requires the highest participation of the adult roles you can choose and should be used when a child is having the greatest difficulty. As the child learns more skills, you can assume a less involved role. The following chart can guide you as you decide which role is more appropriate.

Level of Caregiver Participation			
More			Less
Play Tutoring From the Inside	Play Tutoring From the Outside	Co playing	Parallel Playing

Here are some further guidelines as you think about your role with individual children.

Parallel Play

- Can be used at any time
- Is best with sensorimotor or constructive play
- Will not disrupt play

Co-playing

- Can be used anytime an adult is invited to join play
- Participate as long as children and you are enjoying it
- Will not disrupt play if children remain in control

Play Tutoring

- Can be used when:
  - Children do not engage in make-believe play on their own
  - Children have difficulty playing with other children
  - Children's play is repetitious or appears ready to break down
  - The caregiver is introducing a new play theme
- Can be very disruptive because of adult control; caution should be used
- Should be phased out when play is going well

Adapted from Johnson, Christie, & Yawkey, 1987.

The chart that follows will help you to define roles and decide when each is appropriate.

ROLE OF THE ADULT			
	Definition	**When**	**With Whom**
Parallel Play	Adult plays next to child with same materials, but does not address child directly	Sensorimotor or constructive play	Withdrawn children Children with short attention spans
Co-playing	Adult joins ongoing play and lets children control the direction of the play Adult influences by asking for instructions and responding to children's actions and comments	Any type of material	Children who are repeating a play theme endlessly and seem "stuck" in it Children who already have a high level of play Children with a short attention span
Play Tutoring	Adult begins play Adult assumes partial control Adult teaches new play behaviors Both inside and outside play tutoring are used	Anytime adult can begin play Adult should use materials most attractive to children Can be used to introduce new play theme	Children who do not make-believe, always play alone, or show no progress when an adult uses less intrusive methods Children who show a need for new play skills as shown on the Play Checklist

Adapted from Johnson, Christie, & Yawkey, 1987.

Michael Siluk

CASE STUDIES

We have spent considerable time discussing preparation for play. To illustrate these concepts we have included two case studies. In one, we continue with the planning for Asheley that was begun in Chapter 4. In the second case study, we introduce Willie, a three year old who always wants to be boss.

Asheley

Observations

Asheley was observed four times during free play periods. During these observations, Asheley tended to play with the same materials each day, spending a great deal of her time at the water or sand table. She did not speak to others very often and when she did others had difficulty understanding her. Oftentimes her caregiver needed to help other children know what she was saying, especially when there was a problem sharing a toy. If Asheley used materials to pretend she did one thing with them. For example, she would pat the baby on the back or rock it but then move on to another activity. These observations were used to complete a Play Checklist for Asheley. Her checklist follows.

PLAY CHECKLIST

Date: ____________________

Name: Asheley

Date of Birth: ____________________

Check the highest level skills you consistently observe:

*1. Pretending with Objects

- ☐ Does not use objects to pretend
- ☒ Uses real objects
- ☐ Substitutes objects for other objects
- ☐ Uses imaginary objects

*2. Role-Playing

- ☐ No role play
- ☒ Uses one sequence of play
- ☐ Combines sequences
- ☐ Uses verbal declaration (i.e., "I'm a doctor.")
- ☐ Imitates actions of role, including dress

*3. Verbalizations about Play Scenario

- ☒ Does not use pretend words during play
- ☐ Uses words to describe substitute objects
- ☐ Uses words to describe imaginary objects and actions (i.e., "I'm painting a house.")
- ☐ Uses words to create a play scenario (i.e., "Let's say we're being taken by a monster.")

*4. Verbal Communication during a Play Episode

- ☒ Does not verbally communicate during play
- ☐ Talks during play only to self
- ☐ Talks only to adults in play
- ☐ Talks with peers in play by stepping outside of role
- ☐ Talks with peers from within role (i.e., "Eat your dinner before your dad comes home.")

*5. Persistence in Play

- ☒ Less than five minutes
- ☐ Six to nine minutes
- ☐ Ten minutes or longer

6. Interactions

- ☒ Plays alone
- ☐ Plays only with adults
- ☐ Plays with one child, always the same person
- ☐ Plays with one child, can be different partners
- ☐ Can play with two or three children all together

#7. Entrance to a Play Group

- ☒ Does not attempt to enter play group
- ☐ Uses force to enter play group
- ☐ Stands near group and watches
- ☐ Imitates behavior of group
- ☐ Makes comments related to play theme
- ☐ Gets attention of another child before commenting

8. Conflict Management

- ☐ Gives in during conflict
- ☐ Uses force to solve conflicts
- ☒ Seeks adult assistance
- ☐ Imitates verbal solutions provided by adults
- ☐ Recalls words to use when reminded
- ☐ Initiates use of words
- ☐ Accepts reasonable compromises

9. Turn-Taking

- ☐ Refuses to take turns
- ☐ Leaves toys; protests when others pick them up
- ☒ Gives up toy easily if done with it
- ☐ Gives up toy if another child asks for it
- ☐ Takes turns if arranged and directed by an adult
- ☐ Asks for turn, does not wait for a response
- ☐ Proposes turn taking; will take and give turns

10. Support of Peers

- ☐ Shows no interest in peers
- ☐ Directs attention to distress of peers
- ☒ Offers help
- ☐ Offers and takes suggestions of peers at times
- ☐ Encourages or praises peers

Note: The developmental progression outlined in each segment of the play checklist can be used as a guideline when assessing most children's development. However, not all individuals will go through the same steps in development nor through the same developmental sequence.

Sections marked with * are adapted from: Smilansky, S. 1968. *The Effects of Sociodramatic Play on Disadvantaged Preschool Children.* New York: Wiley

Sections marked with # are adapted from: Hazen, Black, & Fleming-Johnson. "Social Acceptance." *Young Children* 39 (1984): 26-36.

From *Pathways to Play: Developing Play Skills in Young Children.* Redleaf Press, 450 N. Syndicate, St. Paul, MN 55104, 1-800-423-8309.

Goals

When you review Asheley's Play Checklist you will notice she was not using language to communicate during play; her role-playing skills were not well developed; and she had difficulty getting along with the other children. Her caregiver wanted to help Asheley learn to play with others but was unsure where to begin.

It became obvious that Asheley's language skills needed further assessment by someone skilled in this area. The caregiver talked with Asheley's parents and a visit to a language specialist was arranged.

In the child care setting, the caregiver decided to focus on role playing. Her caregiver felt that Asheley's poor pretend skills might be part of the reason Asheley did not comfortably join the play of others. The second area to be prioritized was interactions. Two goals were developed for Asheley:

1. Asheley will combine two sequences of play in two out of three play episodes.
2. Asheley will engage in pretend play with an adult four out of five days a week.

Strategies

1. To work on the goal *"Asheley will combine two sequences of play in two out of three play episodes,"* her caregiver decided to expand her play when she was playing out her favorite themes. She knew that when Asheley did pretend, she chose to dress her favorite doll. She planned to increase the number of times that Asheley played in the housekeeping area by inviting her to join an adult and by offering some new and highly motivating experiences, such as diapering the dolls and feeding them. It was likely that Asheley was familiar with what takes place when caring for a baby because she had a nine month old brother. Asheley needed real objects to use as she played, so real diapers, empty powder containers, bottles, and doll strollers were gathered. This play activity was planned during free play. Asheley's caregiver felt she needed to help Asheley combine sequences using play tutoring from within play. She planned to direct Asheley to diaper the doll and then to feed her.
2. To work on the goal *"Asheley will engage in pretend play with an adult four out of five days a week,"* times were planned for Asheley to play with an assistant teacher with whom she had developed a special relationship. During free play, two days a week, the assistant teacher was to set up a special activity where she and Asheley could work on Asheley's pretend skills. Because Asheley rarely pretended with materials other than those in the housekeeping area, it was important to begin with those materials. For the first week, cleaning the doll house was planned. Materials including a dust cloth, sponge, bucket of water, and other equipment that might be used were gathered before play began.

For Asheley, this was a special time with the assistant teacher so her teachers decided that Asheley and the assistant teacher would be the only ones to work on cleaning the doll house. Duplicate materials would be available for children to use in other areas of the room. The caregiver was to direct her play by using statements like, "Let's pretend to..." She might also ask questions such as, "What should we pretend to clean next?"

On days when Asheley was not working with the assistant teacher, each adult in the classroom would make an effort to spend some time with Asheley during free play. They were to join whatever activity Asheley had chosen. If she wasn't yet pretending they would try to introduce a play idea.

Willie

Observation

Willie is a three-year, nine month old boy that has been in family child care for three months. Willie's schedule is sporadic and he is absent frequently. When he is at child care he is usually in a good mood and easily occupies himself with appropriate play ideas. He plays with a variety of materials, although he most frequently plays in the block or housekeeping area. After observing Willie three times, the caregiver completed the following Play Checklist for him.

PLAY CHECKLIST

Date: ______________________________

Name: Willie

Date of Birth: ______________________________

Check the highest level skills you consistently observe:

*1. Pretending with Objects
- ☐ Does not use objects to pretend
- ☐ Uses real objects
- ☒ Substitutes objects for other objects
- ☐ Uses imaginary objects

*2. Role-Playing
- ☐ No role play
- ☐ Uses one sequence of play
- ☐ Combines sequences
- ☒ Uses verbal declaration (i.e., "I'm a doctor.")
- ☐ Imitates actions of role, including dress

*3. Verbalizations about Play Scenario
- ☐ Does not use pretend words during play
- ☐ Uses words to describe substitute objects
- ☒ Uses words to describe imaginary objects and actions (i.e., "I'm painting a house.")
- ☐ Uses words to create a play scenario (i.e., "Let's say we're being taken by a monster.")

*4. Verbal Communication during a Play Episode
- ☐ Does not verbally communicate during play
- ☐ Talks during play only to self
- ☐ Talks only to adults in play
- ☐ Talks with peers in play by stepping outside of role
- ☒ Talks with peers from within role (i.e., "Eat your dinner before your dad comes home.")

*5. Persistence in Play
- ☐ Less than five minutes
- ☐ Six to nine minutes
- ☒ Ten minutes or longer

6. Interactions
- ☐ Plays alone
- ☐ Plays only with adults
- ☐ Plays with one child, always the same person
- ☐ Plays with one child, can be different partners
- ☒ Can play with two or three children all together

#7. Entrance to a Play Group
- ☐ Does not attempt to enter play group
- ☐ Uses force to enter play group
- ☐ Stands near group and watches
- ☐ Imitates behavior of group
- ☒ Makes comments related to play theme
- ☐ Gets attention of another child before commenting

8. Conflict Management
- ☐ Gives in during conflict
- ☐ Uses force to solve conflicts
- ☐ Seeks adult assistance
- ☐ Imitates verbal solutions provided by adults
- ☒ Recalls words to use when reminded
- ☐ Initiates use of words
- ☐ Accepts reasonable compromises

9. Turn-Taking
- ☐ Refuses to take turns
- ☐ Leaves toys: protests when others pick them up
- ☐ Gives up toy easily if done with it
- ☒ Gives up toy if another child asks for it
- ☐ Takes turns if arranged and directed by an adult
- ☐ Asks for turn, does not wait for a response
- ☐ Proposes turn taking; will take and give turns

10. Support of Peers
- ☐ Shows no interest in peers
- ☐ Directs attention to distress of peers
- ☒ Offers help
- ☐ Offers and takes suggestions of peers at times
- ☐ Encourages or praises peers

Note: The developmental progression outlined in each segment of the play checklist can be used as a guideline when assessing most children's development. However, not all individuals will go through the same steps in development nor through the same developmental sequence.

Sections marked with * are adapted from: Smilansky, S. 1968. *The Effects of Sociodramatic Play on Disadvantaged Preschool Children.* New York: Wiley

Sections marked with # are adapted from: Hazen, Black, & Fleming-Johnson. "Social Acceptance." *Young Children* 39 (1984): 26-36.

From *Pathways to Play: Developing Play Skills in Young Children.* Redleaf Press, 450 N. Syndicate, St. Paul, MN 55104, 1-800-423-8309.

Goals

There were two things that worried Willie's caregiver when she watched him. Her first worry was that although he knew the right words to use when asking for toys, Willie said the words and grabbed the toy at the same time. This upset the other children and caused problems. In the turn-taking section Willie was at the level "Takes turns if arranged and directed by an adult." However, observations indicated that he had difficulty with the next skill listed, "Asks for turn, does not wait for a response." The first goal written for Willie was: *Willie will ask for a turn and wait for a response 50% of the time*.

Secondly, Willie had good play ideas but he usually insisted that play go his way. When other children refused, the play fell apart and he was left to play by himself. A second goal area chosen for Willie was "Support of Peers." On the Play Checklist completed for him, you will see that his current level of functioning in this area is "offers help." He has difficulty with "takes suggestions of peers." The goal that was written for Willie in this area was: *Willie accepts play suggestions of others 25% of the time*.

Strategies

One activity that was arranged to help Willie learn to *ask for a turn and wait for a response 50% of the time*, was to play with playdough. In this activity children usually exchanged materials and there were plenty of opportunities to work with him on turn-taking. The caregiver decided that she would have the children play with playdough at the kitchen table just before lunch. She would encourage Willie to participate. She knew that one of his favorite things to play was "baker," so she suggested that he use the playdough to form muffins, cookies, taffy, or other "edible" objects that a baker might make. While watching Willie play she planned to reinforce him for using words to ask for tools. She would also remind him to wait for a child to respond to his request by saying things like, "Andrew didn't get a chance to answer you. Is it ok for him to use it, Andrew?"

Willie was allowed to bake the items he made in a nearby play oven. Children were free to join the activity and leave it as they wanted. Materials included: playdough, rolling pins, cookie cutters, scissors, muffin tins, and spatulas. The children could also use toothpicks if they requested them.

Willie's caregiver worked on the second goal, *Willie accepts play suggestions of others 25% of the time*, at various times throughout the day. Willie's difficulty accepting suggestions of others usually happened in the housekeeping area. This area was always open for play. When playing house he often insisted on being the father and he was unwilling to play any of the other roles. He also insisted on being the baker whenever the children played bakery and got quite angry when others suggested that he become the customer or the delivery person.

Whenever Willie chose to spend time in the housekeeping area his caregiver moved to that area also. She decided to use play tutoring from outside as she worked on helping him learn to give and take in planning a play theme and determining the roles the children would take. She invited two to three other children to join them when it was appropriate. She knew that as she worked on this she must be ready to help Willie value any of the roles he took on, or roles that were assigned to him. To do this she would expand on them and point out to him their importance to the play. She also planned to help solve any conflicts that arose by listening to all the play ideas and helping the children decide which one to play first.

This lesson plan is difficult because it relies solely on teachable moments. It would be easy to forget to become involved with Willie when he was in the housekeeping area until there was a problem or to forget to work on this goal altogether.

To make it easier to remember, some caregivers write key words or phrases from the goals of a specific child on notes. They post the notes in the play areas where they plan to work with the child. If you decide to do this, be careful to consider confidentiality. Write the reminders in a code that makes sense to you but does not draw the attention of visitors. Other caregivers review goals for children on a daily basis. This helps them to monitor the progress they have made toward a goal and reminds them to continue that focus.

You may be worried that by doing so much planning, the play will lack spark and imagination. In reality, such careful planning and preparation frees you up to interact in a spontaneous way during play.

TIME FOR ACTION

Now you have the information you need to begin a lesson plan for the child you are working with in your setting. As you develop your plan, give attention to your role in working with her. Match your level of involvement to the needs of the child. Give equal attention to the activities you present. In the next chapter we give a myriad of activities that you can choose from. To help you organize your plan, we have included the following form.

PLANNING FORM

Child's Name: ______________________________

GOAL

Who: ______________________________

Does what: ______________________________

How well or how often: ______________________________

Target Completion Date for Goal: ______________________________

LESSON PLAN

Date: ______________________________

When will you work on the lesson? ______________________________

____

What are the child's special interests? ______________________________

____

How many children will be involved? ______________________________

____

Where will the playing take place? ______________________________

____

What props will be needed? ______________________________

____

Your role: ______________________________

____

Activities during play: ______________________________

____

____

Support Strategies: ______________________________

____

____

CHAPTER 6

TEACHING STRATEGIES

Marcie, a teacher in the four-year-olds' room, is planning for the next day. She has observed Estella and completed the play checklist on her. Estella loves to play in the house corner alone, but whenever other children join her, she runs off. Marcie wants to help Estella learn to play with at least one other child. As she reviews her observations, Marcie notes how much Estella enjoys pretending to cook, serving food and doing dishes in the play house. Marcie knows Estella's family, and that they speak Spanish at home and eat a diet of tortillas, rice and beans. Marcie chooses as her first step to serve tortillas as a snack. This will familiarize all the children with tortillas, and they can even cook them during small group time. Then Marcie can encourage Estella to pretend to make tortillas with Marcie, another four year old, during free play time. If all goes well, Marcie can withdraw from the play and watch from the sidelines, available if help is needed.

It was easy for Marcie to establish a goal for Estella, but she had to plan carefully for the activities that would both be interesting and fun, and encourage play skill development. You too may have goals and the start of a plan for an individual child, but you may need activities that will teach the skill and be fun. If you need ideas for activities, this chapter has suggestions to use as part of your plan. These ideas are only a few of the creative ways you can help children learn play skills. Tap into your own playfulness to design an inviting sequence of play.

We have divided this chapter into the following ten sections that correspond to the sections of the Play Checklist and added a Time for Action:

Pretending with Objects
Role-Playing
Verbalizations about Play Scenario
Verbal Communication during a Play Episode
Persistence in Play
Interactions
Entrance to a Play Group
Conflict Management
Turn-Taking
Support of Peers
Time for Action

Under each of the Play Checklist sections, you will find some of the following subsections to help you more fully develop your teaching strategy:

Getting Ready for…
Goals
Suggestions
Support Strategies
Example

Bm Porter/Don Franklin

Getting Ready for...

Eight of the ten sections include information under this heading. Here you will find suggestions for working on prerequisite skills, such as building trust or relationship, that are needed before work on a play skill can begin. Many of these suggestions will help children who are not performing the skills on the checklist. For example, in the section "Verbalization About Play Scenario," the child may not be talking at all during play. Under the "Getting Ready" heading, you can find ways to help the child talk in your setting.

Goals

This section includes examples of goals that have been written using items from the Play Checklist as the core. In Chapter 4 three questions were used in writing goals: The examples in this section answer the question "Does what?" In most sections, goals correspond to the skills sequences listed in the checklist. In a few sections the goals differ from the checklist when one or more items lead to the same goal. Occasionally two closely related goals are listed together.

To individualize the goals presented, substitute the name of the child with whom you are working for "the child" in the example goals. Identify how well the child is currently performing the skill and answer the question "How well or how often?" do you want him to perform the new skill by your target completion date. Remember to move a child slowly and to keep your expectations realistic.

Let's look at one of the example goals presented in the section "Verbal Communication During the Play Episode" to see how to individualize a goal. The goal as it appears in this chapter is: "Child will talk with peers during play." Once individualized it might become:

Who: Sabrina

Does what: will talk with peers during play

How well or how often: one time, three out of four days.

Suggestions

In this section, you will find suggestions for moving a child toward the goals. These may include ways to set up the environment, words to use, and individual or group activities.

During Play

Choose from these activities to give the child opportunities to practice the skill defined in the goal *during play time*. For instance, you might work on a goal directed at improving role-playing skills by bringing in suitcases and dress-up clothes so children can pretend to pack for a trip. Work on a goal about the substitution of objects can be facilitated by providing cardboard boxes to be used as cars or cribs.

In addition to your planned play experiences, some of your work on goals will take place as opportunities arise spontaneously during play. In these situations you will need to respond quickly. For instance, when a child is having difficulty solving a problem, you may take the opportunity to teach her about the words she could use. To make the best use of these "teachable moments" you must have clearly in mind your goals for each child, your verbal responses, and the strategies you plan to use in teaching her.

Support Strategies

Supplement your plans for teaching during play by including activities that help teach skills during group time, story, transitions, table times, or other structured times throughout the day. These are usually more contrived activities than teachable moments. They *support* your work in teaching a skill. Some examples of this are a story about helping others, a discussion of ways to solve a problem, or an art project in which pairs of children share crayons and paper.

Example

An example at the end of each section illustrates a situation in which the suggestions have been used.

Even though you may be working on only one goal at a time, we recommend that you read an entire section. For example, you may be working on the goal: "Child will use substitute objects for other objects." This is found in the first section on "Pretending with Objects." Read all the information in the "Pretending with Objects" section. This information will help you better understand the sequence of the skill development. In addition, some of the activities can be used to teach skills other than just the one under which it is listed.

There may be times that the information will not fit your situation exactly. Because each child is different, you will need to modify the goals and suggestions to make them work for you and the child. Respecting the child's culture, learning style, and temperament should be a primary consideration.

PRETENDING WITH OBJECTS

If a preschooler can only pretend with real objects, that child is limited in sociodramatic play. Unless the child can use substitute objects or imaginary objects, play will go along without him. Pretending with objects is usually one of the first skills a child gains on the play checklist. Therefore if a preschooler cannot pretend with imaginary objects or is heavily dependent on real objects, concentrate on this area.

Getting Ready to Pretend

If a child is not using objects to pretend, you will notice that he uses toys by manipulating, stacking, and pounding them much as a infant would. There will be no pretend play with objects.

It requires careful observation to determine what a child is pretending. You can tell if a child is pretending by observing his actions, listening to his words, and understanding the play theme. If you have a child in your care who is delayed in language, for example, you may not be able to understand the play theme and consequently will miss any pretending that happens. One child was carrying around a block and periodically putting it close to his mouth. This looked like a sensorimotor activity until the teacher saw the child muttering to the block and realized that the child was using the block as a walkie-talkie.

If you have decided that the child is not pretending in play you may need to focus on building a relationship before you can address the first goal. This is especially necessary if the child has emotional issues that are interfering with the development of play skills. It appears to us that pretending requires taking a risk and some children are afraid to do that without a strong relationship with an adult. By building the relationship, you are building the trust that a child needs to risk the world of play.

To build trust:

- Play with the child like parents do with their infants. Use games like chase, hide-and-seek, or peek-a-boo.
- Use puppets to play games with the child. Examples of simple, fun games with puppets include wrestling with the child or hiding behind objects.
- Spend special one-on-one time with the child every day or on a consistent basis.
- As the child's trust in you grows move to the suggestions listed under the first goal.

Goal: Child will use real looking objects to pretend

Suggestions

During Play

- Observe the child closely to determine which toys are favorites.
- Collect a number of these objects and present them to the child. Demonstrate one play sequence at a time with these objects. For example:

With Dolls	With Play Food	With Toy Cars
Feed them	Cook it	Drive them
Dress them	Eat it	Crash them
Hug them	Set table	Put people in them
Comb their hair	Wash dishes	

  Encourage the child to imitate your actions.

- Offer the child the objects and suggest a pretend sequence. For instance, say, "Amy, feed the baby with the bottle."
- Remember that the child probably has not accomplished this goal until he can pretend with real objects spontaneously.

Support Strategies

- During large or small group time, give each child a doll, bottle, and blanket. Talk about how to care for a baby while they act this out with the doll. For example, have them all feed the doll, wrap the doll in the blanket, and rock the doll.
- Choose other themes that the whole group can act out with real objects. Other themes might be:

  How do you care for animals?
  Brush them
  Feed them
  Pet them

  How do you get ready in the morning?
  Brush teeth
  Eat
  Brush hair
  Get dressed

Goal: Child will use substitute objects for other objects

This goal is a bridge between using real objects to using pretend and imaginary objects. You are gradually moving the child from using objects that look very much like the real object to using objects that are less and less similar.

Suggestions

During Play

- Collect a number of props that are similar to the real objects that the child favors. Substitute these objects for the real objects in the dramatic play area. Leave some real objects in the area to encourage play. Some of the substitutions may be:

    Plastic milk bottle for a baby bottle
    Box or block instead of a baby bed
    Block for a milk carton
    Paper for money
    Metal ring for a steering wheel

- As the child plays in the area, sit close by and observe the play activity. If a child seems to be looking for the real object, give him the substitute and say, "You can use this for the baby's bed."
- The child may reject this suggestion by ignoring you or picking up the substitute and then putting it down without using it. You may want to try an object that is more similar to the real object. For example, you are trying to encourage a child to use a block for a bed. If the child will not use it, you could bring out a box with blankets that looks more like a real bed.
- It is fine to go back to the real object if the child is very frustrated with your suggestions.
- Continue introducing substitutes in a relaxed manner. Do not force the child to pretend with substitutes but continue your encouragement.

Support Strategies

- Watch the video *Moving Machines* from Bo-Peep Productions (1989) with your children. This gives children a chance to see real machines at work and observe children pretending with construction toys. Then give your group of children construction toys.

Goal: Child will pretend with imaginary objects

Usually a child moves rather quickly to using imaginary objects once he has mastered substitutions. However, if you find that the child is not doing this naturally, you can help the child.

Suggestions

During Play

- Set up a dramatic play area that emphasizes feeding of food or exchange of money. For example, cooking or buying gas for the car encourages these imaginary actions. These actions are often easier for children because they see them so often.
- Continue observing the child to decide if the child is adding more imaginary actions to his repertoire over time. If not, play with the child and introduce imaginary actions as appropriate.
- Pull back to a co-player role and introduce imaginary actions or objects when the children have already organized their play.

Support Strategies

- Play a modified version of charades in which you act out cleaning, cooking, washing clothes, skating, etc. Have the children guess what you are doing. Encourage the children to perform the imaginary actions as well.
- Use transition times to pretend to skate to the next room or paint an imaginary wall as you walk.
- Act out dramatic play themes during large group using imaginary actions. Some of these might be:

    Driving bus
    Driving car
    Getting ready in the morning
    Baking cookies

- Sing songs with imaginary actions like *Wheels on the Bus* and *This is the Way We Wash Our Clothes.*
- After you have played marching band with real or homemade instruments, create an imaginary marching band. Have each child make the sound and actions from an instrument and march around the room.

Jenny loved to play with the stove and refrigerator in the house area. However, if certain pots and pans were missing, she became quite upset. Other children were happy to use whatever was there. As her caregiver watched her, she noticed that Jenny didn't pretend with anything other than real objects. Without the pots and pans that looked like real objects, Jenny had difficulty playing and became frustrated. The caregiver decided to play with Jenny and a group of children. She brought in a bowl and used it when she cooked. In a few days, she gave the bowl to Jenny and suggested that she use it. At first, Jenny refused to use the bowl. The caregiver did not insist, but within the next week tried again. After a couple of months, she noticed that Jenny was starting to substitute on her own. The caregiver then concentrated on giving Jenny imaginary objects, like pretend food, during play.

ROLE-PLAYING

In theatre, actors take on the voice, costuming, actions, and words appropriate to the roles they are playing. A good actor or actress can be so completely transformed that the audience no longer sees the real person, only the role. This is what children are doing in sociodramatic play. When a child is four to five years old, he should be able to take on a role that includes a spectrum of factors: clothes, voice, speech, and physical actions. Sometimes a child can so effectively mimic the roles of a parent or teacher that it is uncanny to the observer. To learn this role, the child becomes an acute observer of human behavior and translates this understanding into action. This is a big task for a child to learn, one he begins very early in life. The first time a child picks up a telephone and holds it to his ear or pretends to feed a doll, he is beginning to role-play. His understanding of role-playing increases as his experience, cognitive understanding, and observational powers increase.

Getting Ready to Role Play

If the child doesn't role-play in your setting, determine if the child role plays in other settings such as at home or with familiar friends. If he does, you know that the child can role play but is not doing it with you. Your task is to encourage the child to risk this behavior with you and his peers in the child care setting. Sometimes the child may be afraid to take this risk. If you are dealing with a withdrawn or shy child who does not take risks with you, do not push or be direct in your requests. Try the following:

Suggestions

During Play

- Suggest a role for the child that is not central to the play. For instance, the child could be a baby with little language.
- Allow the child to observe play from outside the group for awhile.
- Quietly give the child a role in play that requires little risk. For example, in a pizza restaurant, the child could put paper pepperonis on pizzas.
- Do not bring too much attention to the child's efforts to play a role. Be encouraging but with smiles, hugs, or indirect comments rather than direct praise.

Bm Porter/Don Franklin

Another reason a child may not role play is that he does not understand the role you are asking him to play. Look at the child's experience. Does he know what a firefighter or police officer does? Most likely, even if the child lacks understanding of the proposed role, he will be able to play other, more familiar roles. If the child does not understand the role:

Suggestions

During Play

- Play with the child, demonstrating what adults do when they are in this role in real life.

Support Strategies

- Plan a field trip so that the child can observe how adults perform in that role.
- Read a book about the role in the community.
- Bring people like firefighters, naturalists, zookeepers, and police officers to your setting to share what they do in their jobs.

Goal: Child will pretend one sequence of play

Usually a young toddler begins pretending one sequence of play with familiar toys like dolls, trucks, and telephones.

Suggestions

During Play

- Use props that are familiar to the child like telephones, food, dolls, pots and pans, trucks and cars.
- Use real objects rather than more abstract props. To begin with, play sessions should be just the child and an adult.
- Model the one sequence, then include the child after you have finished the sequence. For example, talk on the telephone, then hand the phone to the child saying, "It's for you."
- If the child is able to pretend with one prop, begin other sequences with new props until you feel confident that the child is ready to move to the next stage.

Support Strategies

- During transitions, pretend to be a bird or an animal.
- Play other games with the child that encourage playfulness like hide-and-seek, peek-a-boo, and chase.
- During large group time act out short sequences like popcorn popping, seeds growing, or taking off in a rocket ship.

Goal: Child will combine sequences of play

Suggestions

During Play

- Bring props that are related to one another, like pots and pans and dishes or a doll and a bottle and a blanket.
- As you did with the one sequence of play, model two sequences. For instance, feed the doll a bottle and then wrap it in the blanket. If the child does the action after you, give him praise or comment on what he is doing.
- Use different props as the child grows more confident.

Support Strategies

- Act out simple nursery rhymes. You can recite the rhymes while the children perform the actions using simple props. Some nursery rhymes that encourage acting are:

  Jack Be Nimble
  Cat and the Fiddle
  Jack and Jill
  Humpty Dumpty
  Little Jack Horner

Goal: Child will play out all parts of role including dress, speech, and actions

At first when a child is working on this, he may be able to sustain the role only for a short time or use only a limited number of actions or words. As the child gains in this skill, you will see more complexity developing.

Occasionally, you may see a child who states his role verbally, "I'm a doctor," and then runs off. In that case, you may need to help the child understand what a doctor does. Modeling is often very effective with such a child.

Suggestions

During Play

- Play a birthday party and have the child blow out candles, open pretend presents, and wear a birthday hat.
- The child may enjoy role playing an animal such as a cat or dog at first as these involve less language and dress.

- Model a role within play with the child beside you. Suggest that he try it.
- Have different dress-up clothes available with a mirror to encourage role exploration.
- Set up a train with boxes or blocks. Collect props to use with the train like tickets, paper money, and a bell or whistle. One child plays the engineer, one child can be the conductor and collect the tickets, another child can ring the bell or whistle. The rest of the children can ride the train. Other variations on this theme could be travelling on a plane or bus (Wolfgang, Mackender, & Wolfgang, 1981).
- Collect a number of props that are organized into boxes and categories according to a play theme. Some of these props can be stored together in boxes (prop boxes); other, larger props can be kept in a storeroom. Prop boxes, once they are organized, can facilitate sociodramatic play in your setting. They save time, are easy to use and can accommodate additions and elaborations when your children are ready. Following is a chart with possible play themes and the props that could be included:

Dramatic Play Themes	Materials to Include
Airport	Travel posters, suitcases, chairs for inside the airplane, tickets, trays for food, block for walkie-talkie, hats for pilots, hats for flight attendants, etc.
Pizza Parlor	Empty pizza boxes, box for delivery truck, order pads, menu, paper or play food, play dough with paper pepperoni and green peppers, stove or oven, cash register, play money, hats and aprons, etc.
Laundromat	Doll and dress-up clothes, clothespins, boxes for washers and driers, play money, tools, magazines, empty detergent box, measuring cup, laundry basket, etc.
Camping	Tents, canteen, flashlight, blocks for fire, rocking boat for fishing, fishing poles, play fish, backpack, dishes, play food, sleeping bags, etc.
Bakery	Muffin tins, stove, rolling pin, hats, playdough, cookie cutters, cash register, numbers for customers, play money, etc.
Fire Station	Hats, boots, coats, hoses, blocks to build houses, steering wheel, walkie-talkies, cardboard boxes for trucks
Restaurant	Menus, plates, silverware, ordering pad, pencils, cash register, play food, money, hats, aprons, placemats, tables and chairs, etc.
Doctor	White lab coats, doctor kit, gauze, ace bandages, bed or cot, tongue depressors, medicine bottles, chairs, tables and magazines for the waiting room, clipboard and paper, pencils, old X-rays, etc.
House	Refrigerator, stove, cabinets, sink, dress-up clothes, dolls, doll clothes, mirror, dishes, play food, silverware, etc.

- Create a marching band using instruments you have made or commercial instruments. You can march around the room or down halls (Wolfgang, Mackender, & Wolfgang, 1981).
- Set up a moving day. Tell the children that you have to move the house. Provide boxes for packing. Pack the boxes in a wagon and have children work together moving the boxes and the furniture. Then have children join in to unpack and set up in the new house (Wolfgang, Mackender, & Wolfgang, 1981).

Support Strategies

- Act out a story during large group with assigned roles for the children. First read the story to the children, and then discuss it with them. Assign the roles for the children to act out as you narrate the story. This is known as *thematic fantasy play* (Johnson, Christie, & Yawkey, 1987). Act out the story many days in a row so that the children grow familiar with the roles. Let the children take on more of the roles as they grow more comfortable. Some good stories for this are:

  The Three Bears
  Three Billy Goats Gruff
  Caps for Sale
  The Three Pigs
  The Carrot Seed

- Put a story corner in your environment during free play. Let the children act out the story used in the previous suggestion as part of the choice time.
- Provide a flannelboard with flannelboard figures of the stories you have acted out during free play. The children can act out the story using the figures (Wolfgang, Mackender, & Wolfgang, 1981).

> Billy remained apart from the group of children that always played in the house corner. Sometimes he would play with Legos or blocks, but other times he would just look longingly at the involved play in the house area. The teacher decided to set up a pizza restaurant next to the house. The first day the restaurant was open, Billy came over and announced, "I'm the pizza driver man." Then he ran off and left the area completely. He went to the puzzles and sat down. The teacher realized that he may not have known what to do next. She brought him over to the restaurant and asked if he would like to play. He nodded. She gave him a hat and suggested that he deliver the pizza to the house as she handed him a pizza box. He went over to the house and delivered the pizza. Billy spent the rest of free play delivering pizzas. The next day, the teacher drew him into the restaurant as the cashier and a person preparing the pizza. In each case, she gave him suggestions about the role. Although he still wasn't connecting with the other children to a great extent, he was able to play out several roles within the play.

VERBALIZATIONS ABOUT PLAY SCENARIO

Sociodramatic play cannot keep going without words. Language is the glue that holds the play *and* the players together. In this section we discuss how a child's words let other children know what he is pretending. Language brings other children into a shared vision of what the play scene is. You can tell from many actions what a child is imagining. But the words give us a better picture of the child's intentions. Then other children not only understand what the child is doing, but they can join in and add numerous variations. Most children use words to communicate about their pretend play, but some children may use other means. For instance, children who are deaf may use sign language in much the same way as children with hearing use spoken language to label their substitute and imaginary actions. The suggestions we discuss involve spoken language, but we encourage you to adapt the information to your particular children.

Getting Ready to Verbalize About the Play Scenario

In order to use words in sociodramatic play, a child has to be able to use language throughout the day. If you have a child who is not using words at all during play, look closely at how the child uses language during other activities. The lack of words during play may actually point to a more pervasive language problem. If the child is not talking, is unable to express himself, or cannot understand directions, you may need to refer the child to a speech therapist for an evaluation. Hatten and Hatten (1981) give the following list as a guideline in their book *Natural Language*. If you see the following behaviors, consider a referral:

- the child does not speak any words by eighteen months
- the child is not using any two-word combinations by twenty-seven months
- the child is not easily understood most of the time by thirty-six months
- the child is not using short sentences to communicate by thirty-six months
- the child is not totally understandable by forty-eight months
- the child does not speak sentences that sound almost adult-like by forty-eight months

Adapted from Hatten & Hatten, 1981

Although a speech therapist uses speech and language strategies to help a child who has a language delay, caregivers can also do many things in their settings to help the child gain more skill in language. After the child has a better use of words, you can focus on language goals during sociodramatic play.

Suggestions

- Use speech and language stimulation techniques with the child.

  1. Model language during the day.

     Talk to the child throughout the day. Children learn to talk from hearing language around them. Use many kinds of sentences with simple words.

  2. Expand the child's statement.

     Expand what the child says, so that it is slightly more complex. For example, the child says, "More." You can say, "Johnny wants more juice." You are giving the child a little more than what he said. Do not expect the child to imitate you at first, as this may come slowly.

  3. Talk to yourself.

     When you are engaged in activities, talk about what you are doing. This can be uncomfortable at first, but it is a valuable model for the child. Remember these simple rules:

     Keep it simple and short.
     Describe what you are seeing.
     Describe what you are doing.
     Describe what you are thinking.

     Hatten & Hatten, 1981

     Remember that the child will not often repeat after you, so you may not immediately see results.

  4. Talk about what the child is doing.

     As the child plays, describe what the child is doing in short and simple sentences. By doing this, you are supporting the thought process of the child. This is where language first starts. You may be watching a child play with a truck. You could say, "Here comes the truck. I'm driving the truck along the road. It's going around the curve. Whoops. It crashed into the wall."
     Hatten & Hatten, 1981

- Reward all attempts to speak. Even if you do not understand the child, smile and respond. It is important that you do not correct the child when he is attempting to speak. Model the correct sentence but do not expect him to imitate it (Hatten & Hatten, 1981).

- If a child is gesturing but not speaking, say the words along with the child's gestures.

- Concentrate on language during play.

  1. Use all of the speech and language techniques during play as well as during the rest of the day.

  2. Get two telephones and play "talking on the telephones" with the child. Let the children talk to one another.

  3. Do turn-taking activities to encourage the conversational pauses and responses. For example, do an activity and then say, "Your turn." Or roll a ball back and forth. Use your imagination to think of other ways to take turns.

  4. Encourage the child to yell or call out words during gym or outside time. This will loosen the child up so he is willing to take more risks.

- Do language games at group times.

  1. Organize a "following directions" game. Give the child a set of one to three directions depending on how much the child can do at a time. Then have him give you directions.

  2. Introduce a game of "whisper tube" in a large or small group. Collect cardboard tubes from toilet paper and paper towels. Give one to each child. Have them whisper a message to the child next to them. Have the last child in the line report what he heard.

  3. Play hand-clapping imitation games. As the child learns to imitate you, clap different rhythms that he can copy.

  4. Use a record or a song and encourage the children to march, play musical instruments, or do other body activities in time to the music.

  5. Do games and activities that use sound. Part of learning to speak is learning to listen to sounds around you.

     Fill glasses with water to different levels and let the child tap the glasses lightly with a spoon. Decide together which is highest and lowest.

Make a tape of different sounds around your setting, such as a door shutting, people whispering, people walking. Have the child identify the sounds.

Play a number of different musical instruments while hiding behind a wall or a shelf.

Have the children guess which instruments you are playing. Another variation on this game is to have two of each instrument. Have the children guess which instruments are the same and which are different as you play them in sets of twos.

Play blind man's bluff with a bell. Blindfold the child. Ring a bell in different parts of the room. Have the child point to the direction of the sound. (Wolfgang, Mackender, & Wolfgang, 1981).

Play musical chairs with the group of children. Before you play this more complicated game, do many stop-and-go games with music, that is, move to the music and freeze when the music stops. (Don't eliminate children when you play musical chairs, though. Allow everyone to continue to play.)

6. Play games with the child such as 1-2-3-upsey daisy, pat-a-cake, pop goes the weasel, ring-around the rosie, and peek-a-boo. Encourage the child to say more and more of the words with you. During group times ask the children to do the games with each other in pairs.
7. Recite simple nursery rhymes such as *Humpty Dumpty, Little Boy Blue,* or *Old King Cole.*
8. Do finger plays such as *Five Little Monkeys, Itsy Bitsy Spider,* or *Twinkle Twinkle Little Star*. Rhymes with gestures help the child with language and other delays to participate and feel included even if he can't keep up verbally. The gestures also reinforce the learning of the words.

There are many other language games and activities listed in resource books. We encourage you to continue adding to the ideas listed above.

Goal: Child will use words to describe substitute objects

Goal: Child will use words with imaginary objects or imaginary actions

If the child is able to use language at other times of the day, you can help the child use words during play. If the child is not pretending with imaginary objects, the descriptions will be of the substitutions the child is making with objects or substances. A child may pour water into a bowl and say, "It's milk." To describe an imaginary action, the child may hold an imaginary hose with both hands and yell,"I'm putting out the fire!" The verbal description is even more needed when the child is using imaginary objects or actions. The words give the play partners a shared starting point.

Suggestions

During Play

- Play with the child and model descriptions of the substitutions you are making. When rolling out playdough, say, "Here's some cookie dough. Here, you want a cookie?"
- When a child can describe substitute objects, play with the child and model descriptions of imaginary objects and actions. You can pretend to feed the baby with imaginary soup and say, "Oh, baby, doesn't this soup taste good?" Or you can pretend to build a house with blocks and imaginary hammer and nails. As you pretend to pound the nails, you can say, "I'm pounding these nails in good. This is hard work to pound these nails in with the hammer."
- Describe the child's actions as the child is feeding the baby or driving the car.
- Sit next to the child during free play. When the child is involved in play and makes a substitution or demonstrates an imaginary action, provide the words for the child. You see a child give another child pretend money. You say, "Here's some money." There is one caution. The only way you know what the child is pretending is by observing the actions. You need to understand the play theme before you begin your comments.
- Sit beside the child during play and ask the child about his actions. When a child is holding the pretend hose aiming it at the blocks, ask him, "Tell me about your idea." Avoid questions that only require a "yes" or "no" answer.

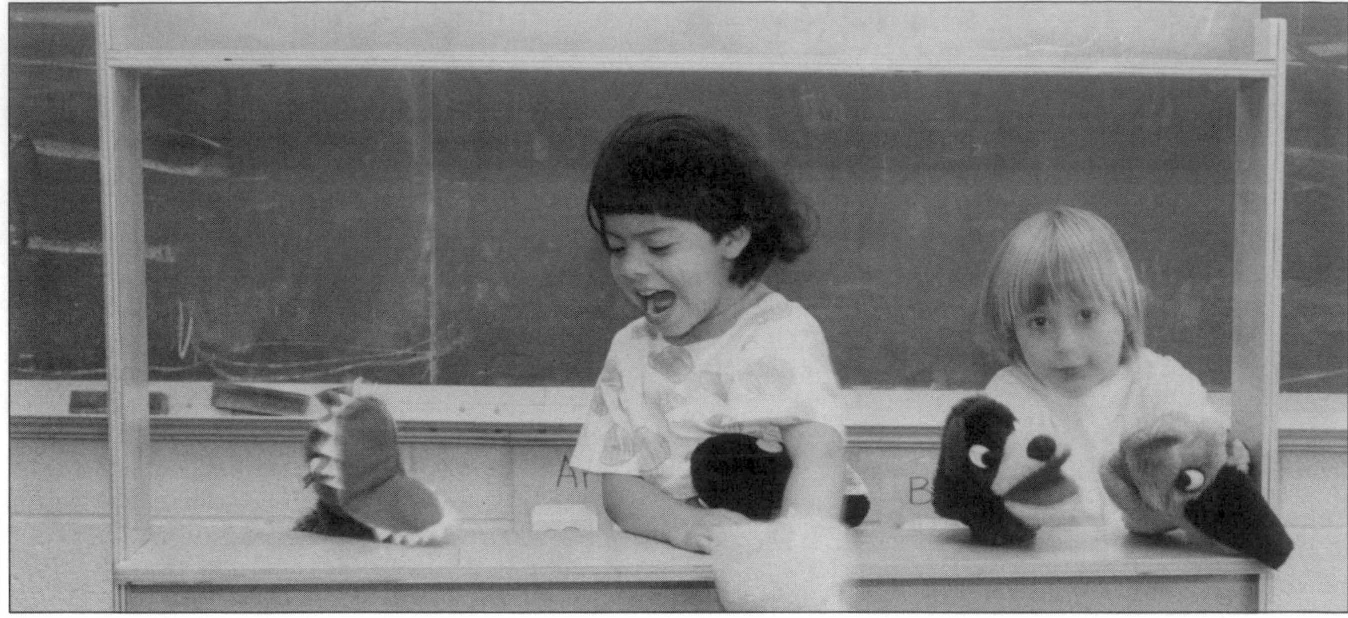
Michael Siluk

- Sit beside the child during free play and ask questions that clarify what the child is doing. When a child is writing with a finger, you say, "It looks like you're writing. What are you writing about?" or, "Tell me about your writing."

Support Strategies

- Do a puppet show of a favorite play theme in your classroom like doctor or firefighting. As the puppets act out the theme, have them talk about their imaginary actions. These should be simple statements like, "Here's my hose. Let's put out the fire."

Goal: Child will use words to create a play scenario

This goal requires a sophisticated understanding of and ability to use language. The child must see pictures in his mind and then use language to create that picture for others. Another child who is highly verbal and skilled at describing a play scene may be a great teacher for the child working on this goal.

Suggestions

During Play

- Create a play scene with props that are clearly defined. For example, set up a rocking boat with fishing poles. Ask the child what he wants to pretend.
- Pair the child with a highly verbal child to play in a separate room set up for dramatic play. Ask clarifying questions as they begin to play. Be careful not to break the flow of the play.
- Create a scenario that draws children into the play. Begin your scene with, "Let's pretend..." As suggestions from the children are added, bring in more props.
- Sit by the child during play and ask questions that will define a scenario choice. For instance, the child may be putting a baby to bed. You can ask, "Is it nighttime or nap time?"
- Ask questions that continue the scenario. Some of these questions are:

  Now that you are done with the nap, what comes next?

  What would your mom do after she set the table?

  What else would a doctor do to a patient?

- Use a co-player role and ask the child what he wants you to do next as you play together.

Support Strategies

- Create a puppet show where the puppets can't decide together on a play scene. The story line could go something like this:

  Two puppets come out and are bored. They want to play something, but what? One puppet says, "Let's pretend we're monsters and are stomping in the snow." The other puppet says, "No." Then the puppet describes a different play scene, "Let's pretend we're ghostbusters running away from some ghosts." But that is not agreeable either. These alternating play scenes could go on for awhile and get sillier and sillier. To resolve it, the puppets could agree on elements from several play scenes or just get so silly they decide to play baseball.

> Antonio was always at the house corner during free play and smiled as children talked about mommies and daddies and babies around him. He would cook at the stove or set the table, but would never say a word. Often the play would go on around him. He was in the middle of the play but not really included. Amy, his caregiver, watched him carefully throughout the day and noted that he would talk a little during gym time or small group time, but was never highly verbal. Although Amy was concerned about how he was left out during play, she decided to concentrate on increasing his language usage during the day. She expanded any words he spoke and described his actions during the day. When he communicated with gestures, she gave the words. Gradually, he began to talk more. Amy kept trying these language techniques, especially during play, confident that Antonio would use his new-found skills to communicate.

VERBAL COMMUNICATION DURING A PLAY EPISODE

Once a group of children has begun a play theme, they require language to keep it going or to change it. This communication can take two forms. A child can communicate about play by talking to the other children from within his role. Such comments are pretend statements that fit within the role the child has chosen. A child who is a patient may say, "I'm really sick. My stomach hurts. Can you help me?" The second way a child communicates is from outside the role. The child breaks the flow of the play to organize the play. These comments can be used to:

talk about pretend objects
"Let's pretend that this box is a car, okay?"

assign roles
"You be the doctor and I'll be the sick one."

plan where the play is going
"First, we'll eat dinner, then we'll go to the movies."

correct players who are not playing the role the right way
"That's not the way dogs act."

Johnson, Christie, & Yawkey, 1987.

We have included only one goal in this section, but we discuss three other situations that are common. First, you may observe a child who does not talk to anyone during play. Second, you may see a child who talks only to himself. This child may just babble to no one in particular.

Third, you may have a child in your care who talks only with adults in play. Unless the communication flows between children, the play will be too dependent on adults.

Getting Ready to Verbally Communicate During a Play Episode

In this section, as in Verbalizations about the Play Scenario, a child will be less able to verbally communicate in play if he has an overall language delay. To address this, refer to the suggestions to help a child gain language skills. (Page no. 56)

Occasionally, a child will talk easily during play, but will address these comments to no one in particular. This is called self-talk. The child describes what he is doing, thinking, or intending. When children are learning to talk, this skill is very valuable. Eventually these verbalizations become part of an adult's silent thinking process. However, when a child is playing in a group and *only* talks to himself the words do nothing to build bridges between players. This child is often ignored or left behind. Self-talk is not a concern if the child occasionally prefers to talk to himself when playing rather than to peers. It is a concern if the child chooses to talk only to himself and does not connect with other children.

Suggestions

During Play

- Sit close to the child during play. As the child talks, make comments that connect the child to other players. The child may be saying, "I'm pouring milk into the bottle. Be quiet, baby. I'll feed you." Say to the child, "Daniel, ask Jamie to hold the baby while you're getting the milk ready." One of the tricky parts of your role is knowing how to get into the play without interrupting the flow of the group. Keep your comments short and simple. If the child ignores you, do not press your point. Just keep trying at future times.

- If the other children are ignoring the child even when he is trying to communicate with them, you can say, "Jamie, Daniel is asking for help with his baby."

Some children have excellent verbal skills but do not choose to talk with peers in play. However, they immediately pull in an adult when one is near. They will direct all play comments to the adult but will ignore the children. To help this child, the adult should use this central role to pull other children into the play. As connections are made between the players, you should physically distance yourself from the play to observe. If the play falls apart, you can go in again to add props or present a new play theme to the group.

As a child improves his communication with his peers, he may be reluctant to speak with the other children if he cannot be easily understood. Children may not understand him or be so busy playing they don't give the child time to finish sentences. Sometimes children will comment on how the child talks with brutal honesty. They may say, "Jerod talks funny." Or "Jane doesn't say that word right." These comments can inhibit a child from making attempts to communicate.

Although you may be uncomfortable with the children's honesty about the child's language problems, it is best to treat the subject calmly and openly. Explain to the children that sometimes Jerod can't say the word clearly so we need to listen carefully. Tell them that Jerod is learning to speak more clearly. Point out things that Jerod does well like running or riding a trike. Show how we all have things to learn and things that we do well. If they are having trouble understanding Jerod, they should come to you for help.

Goal: Child Will Talk with Peers During Play

At the beginning of this section, we discussed the ways children talk during play. They either talk from within the role, making comments that are appropriate to the role, or they interrupt the play momentarily to organize the play. In the goal above either of these ways of communicating can be addressed. It is ideal if the child achieves a balance between these two types of communication.

Suggestions

During Play

- Suggest that the child make requests and direct comments to other children. The adult can say, "Tell Jeremy that he can come to dinner."
- Direct other children's attention to the child's comments if they do not respond.
- Give the child the words to use when he is talking to other children. This will be especially necessary if the child has been hesitant to use language. For example, the child is setting the table and another child is cooking at the stove. You can suggest, "Jake, tell Darnell, 'You can serve the supper now.'"
- Pair the child with a partner and plan a special play theme for just the two of them. A child who has been shy about using words will more easily begin with only one child.
- Suggest that the child play a role that requires only a little verbal interaction like a dog or cat, a driver of the bus, or a carpenter. Many of these roles use more physical action and mouth noises than words.

Support Strategies

- Use cardboard tubes in a large group to start a whisper game. Each child has to whisper a message through the tubes to another child (Wolfgang, Mackender, & Wolfgang, 1981).
- Encourage the child to call another child on the play phone and talk, even if briefly.
- Ask the child to talk to puppets manipulated by other children. You may need to give words to the child at first.
- Play Simon Says and after you have played the leadership role, ask the child to lead the group with your help.
- Play a movement game where each child has to copy the leader. Share the leader position so that each child gets a turn.
- Play a game similar to the one above using noises. You make a noise like "shsh" and ask the children to copy it. Again, give each child a turn to lead.
- Do lotto games where children in the group are able to play the leader who announces the pictures.
- Do small group murals where each child paints part of the picture. Talk about each child's part.
- Do a "Star of the Week." Have each child bring his favorite toys, pictures, and clothes from home. During group time each child can explain their special possessions.

Shanita sought out the dramatic play area during free choice time. She was always running to put out fires, set the table, or ride on the bus. Darius, her teacher, saw that she never talked, even though she performed all the appropriate actions. The other children would leave her out as they moved to a new play theme. Although Shanita would move along with the group, she seemed on the outside of the play. Darius decided to sit near the area and give Shanita words that would connect her to the play of the other children. The first day Darius and the children set up a bus with blocks and the steering wheel. Shanita was waiting in line to get on the bus. When it was her turn, Darius said to Shanita, "Shanita, ask the bus driver how much you need to pay." Shanita repeated, "How much?" The bus driver said, "Five cents." She pretended to give the bus driver the money and got on the bus. After a few minutes she got up. Darius said, "Shanita, tell the bus driver you want to get off." Shanita said, "I want off now." The bus driver said, "Okay, you can get off." She stepped out of the bus and smiled broadly. Darius continued to give her words to say throughout the play period. Although she wasn't speaking on her own yet, she was learning that using words in play can bring more response and involvement from other children.

PERSISTENCE IN PLAY

Being able to play for an extended period of time helps a child develop many of the skills needed for play. When children can play only for a few minutes, the group barely has a chance to set up the play, much less develop a theme. The age of the child often determines how long a child can sustain play in a group. A child of four should be able to persist at least five minutes, and a child of five or six should be able to persist for ten minutes (Johnson, Christie, & Yawkey, 1987).

Getting Ready to Persist in Play

Although the goal in this section is to increase the child's time *in sociodramatic play*, many children who cannot stay with play also have short attention spans in other activities as well. If this is the case, you need to also lengthen their attention spans outside of group play.

Intensive play sessions with you or another adult are a good starting point to build longer attention spans. Playing next to or with an adult will often keep children at an activity longer. Once the child's ability to stay with a task has increased, you can begin addressing the goal within sociodramatic play. Following are activities and suggestions that will help the child increase his attention span:

Suggestions

During Play

- Play next to the child in parallel play.
- Plan a play sequence with you and the child that combines sensorimotor activity and dramatic play. Some ideas are:
  Washing babies
  Feeding dolls with beans, playdough, etc.
  Building roads in sand and driving to the store
  Cooking with playdough
  Making pizza with playdough
  Washing cars (trikes) outside
- When the child is doing an activity and begins to leave, ask him to do one more thing. For instance, if the child is doing a puzzle, and begins to leave before he is finished, ask him to put one more piece into the puzzle.
- Hold back props to introduce as the child begins to lose interest. For example, have towels available to dry wet babies or add small plastic animals to the block or sand play.

Support Strategies

- Minimize the number of distractions to the child throughout the day. Look at your environment. Use a limited number of props in the play areas. Do not use too many colors or pictures on the walls. Keep the noise level in the room down. When you limit distractions in such ways, you are helping a child who has difficulty concentrating.
- Comment positively when a child displays a long attention span.
- Provide adult support as often as possible. This will tend to keep a child involved in any activity a little longer.

Goal: Child will engage in sociodramatic play for...minutes

Occasionally, a child will be able to play for a long time when alone with his favorite activity but will not be able to play for long in a group of children. If this describes a child in your care, you can use the following suggestions to help him play longer in a group. These suggestions will also help a child who has a short attention span throughout the day.

Suggestions

During Play

- Choose one or two other children whom the child enjoys. Organize a new play theme for them. This would be especially effective in a separate room where there are fewer distractions. Playing doctor, riding a bus, or playing restaurant can be good themes to start with.

- In the beginning, play with the group to establish theme and roles. If the child starts to leave the group, encourage him to do something new. For example, you are playing doctor and you are pretending you are the patient and the child is the doctor. He is just examining you and he begins to wander off. You can say, "Oh doctor, I think I have a temperature. Will you take my temperature?" When he starts to wander off again, bring in another patient who has a stomachache.

- Hold back a few props to introduce as interest flags. For example, as you play doctor, bring out a doll and bandages as children become restless.

- Choose play themes for groups of children that combine sensorimotor play and dramatic play. Ideas for these play themes were listed previously when we discussed increasing a child's attention span.

- If the child is staying in the group for play, reduce your direct involvement in the play, but stay close by. Continue making suggestions, comments, and questions to maintain interest in the play theme.

Mary could play for hours alone with Lego blocks, puzzles or art projects. She would occasionally join with an adult on the playground if she was playing car wash with the trikes, but if other children joined in, she would wander away. Margaret, the family child care provider, was concerned about this. She decided that she wanted to increase the time Mary would play in a group of children. She had observed that Mary enjoyed any play with water. One morning she took all the doll clothes out and invited Mary and two other children to wash clothes with her. She asked Mary to set up the scrubbing brushes and put soap in the water. She provided only one bucket to wash in so that the children would be together as they washed the clothes. The three children scrubbed the clothes in the water and soap. Mary started to leave after a few minutes. Margaret asked her to help her set up the rinse bucket. Mary enjoyed rinsing a few clothes and started to leave again. Margaret showed her how to hang up the clothes. By this time, Mary had played with the group for at least ten minutes. Throughout the next few weeks, she planned activities for two or three children that used water. Mary began to wander off less and needed fewer suggestions to stay in the play.

INTERACTIONS

To prepare for the group aspect of sociodramatic play children must learn to interact with one another. Group times arranged by the adult help the children to become acquainted as do the informal contacts made by the children themselves. Children who are skilled in getting to know others and interacting have usually had successful relationships with adults, played in pairs, and learned to coordinate their behavior with other players. Interacting with others strengthens the child's ability to communicate and think (Hazen, Black, & Fleming-Johnson, 1984).

Sometimes a child will isolate himself and play alone. Playing alone may be appropriate for infants and toddlers or even very young preschoolers. It becomes a concern, however, when an older child seems unable to make connections with others. A child who consistently does this may not have interaction skills which are developed enough for him to play successfully with others.

Caregivers sometimes hesitate to encourage a child to interact when he appears to like playing alone. We suggest observing the child often enough to determine if he is alone due to a lack of skill development or because of a preference. Look also to see if the child seems to be anxious about his inability to interact. If he appears to be upset or looks as if he wants to join the others but does not know how, use the information that follows to teach the child the skills he needs. When you know the child has the skills and yet chooses to play alone, you can feel assured that he has truly made a choice.

Goal: Child will play with adult

Very young children need positive, successful interactions with adults in which they learn some of the skills they need to interact with their peers. Older children who are having difficulty with interactions also need to return to this first playmate.

Suggestions

During Play

- Share a joke, silly action or funny activity.
- Follow the child's lead in play situations. Do what he suggests or copy some of his behaviors. Use parallel play to build trust and demonstrate that you value what he does as well as the ideas he has.
- Arrange a time each day when you play near the child. Be available to interact with him.

Support Strategies

- Build your relationship with the child by finding out about the child's likes and dislikes. Ask him or ask his parents about his favorite toys, games, and activities. This helps to provide a link between home and the child care setting.
- Visit the child at home. This can be difficult to arrange with busy schedules but in many situations is worthwhile. When you visit a child in his home he is sometimes more comfortable and outgoing. You may get an indication of what he is capable of more quickly than in the child care setting.

Goal: Child will play with one other child, may be the same person

Goal: Child will play with different play partners

As children grow older they begin to switch their attention from the adults they know to the children they are around frequently. After a child

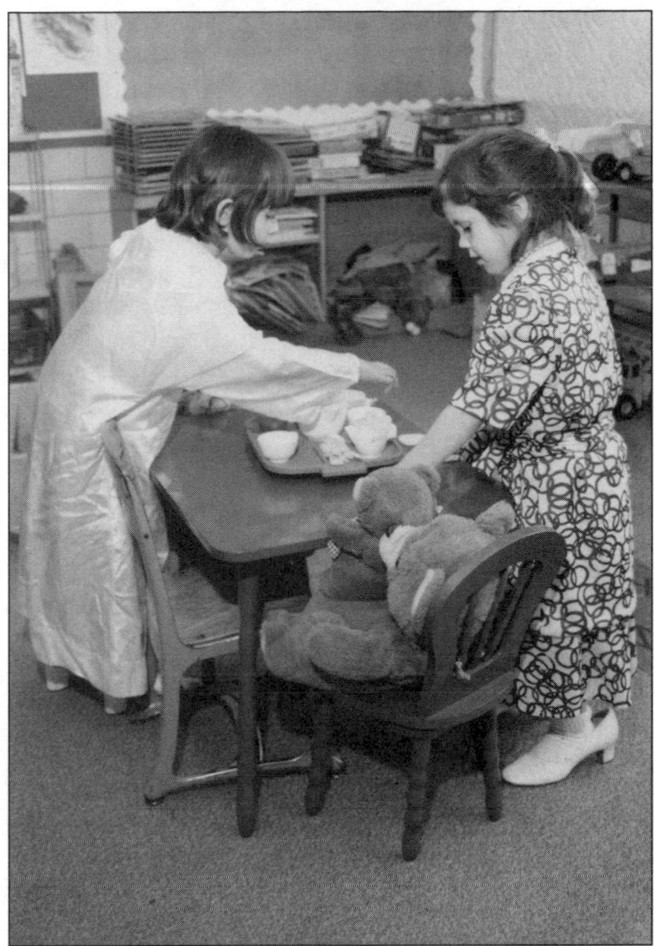
Bm Porter/Don Franklin

has had many opportunities to interact with an adult, encourage activities in which more time is spent in child-to-child contacts than in adult-to-child interactions. For some children, beginning to interact with other children is a slow process. When you first start to encourage child-to-child interactions, it may appear to the child that you are pushing him away. If he perceives it this way, he will be more likely to cling to you.

Suggestions

During Play

- Arrange times when the child can be involved in pretend play with one other child. Find out what he likes to pretend when he plays alone. Look for ways to include the other child. If he likes to build roads in the sand, ask the other child to dig a lake next to the road. Then they can both drive their cars around the lake.
- Take on a role and direct the scenario. You can invite other children to join the play by assigning roles that are compatible. For instance if you are playing race car, you might ask another child to pump gas into your car.

- Phase out your involvement as the children begin to interact appropriately.

Support Strategies

- Point out ways the child is similar to others in the group. Notice very simple things such as similarities in shoe color or that two children have the same first letter in their name. Pay particular attention to times when the child is playing the same thing as other children and comment on it.
- Watch for times when the child is playing next to another child and comment on how he is playing near his friend. Refer to the children in the group as friends. Say things like, "take a friend's hand and walk with us to the bathroom." This helps him to learn about the word friend and helps him to feel as if he can make friends.
- Pair the children for certain activities. Assign the child who has difficulty interacting to work with another child who is likely to accept him. He is more likely to get along easily with someone who is like him in activity level, temperament, and behavior (Rubin, 1980). Paired activities can include finger painting, running errands, doing puppet plays, and telling stories to a tape recorder.
- Be aware of informal contacts children make on their own. Do not interrupt or draw the children's attention away. For example, if two children are counting crackers at snack time, don't interrupt their interaction to ask them how many girls are sitting at the table.

Goal: Child will play with two or three children all together

To interact with two or three children at one time, a child must learn to coordinate his behaviors and see ways that his ideas fit with others.

Suggestions

During Play

- Help children to see that what they are playing fits with what others are doing. Weave story lines that include a number of children. In one family child care home, Gabriel, Allen and Amanda, all four year olds, were playing in the building area. Gabriel had the school, Allen the barn, and Amanda the house. Although they were all near each other, they were playing without much interaction. James got out the school bus and wanted to join them. When the provider asked how they might all play together James thought they might have some people ride his bus. The other children were not too excited about the idea until the adult helped to tie the play themes together with a story. She told how the children woke up in their beds one morning excited about going to school that day because they were going on a field trip to the farm. The children were able to play out the story for about ten minutes before Amanda decided to play elsewhere. The next day the children set up the same play and told the story again.
- Teach the child to respond each time another child talks to him. It is not important that he agrees with the statement or complies to the request but that he responds. "Popular" children acknowledge the comments made by other children whether they agree with the statements or not (Hazen, Black, & Fleming-Johnson, 1984).
- Help the child focus on each player in the group for short periods of time. Children who are successful in groups tend to divide their time between the players. This seems to reduce their chances of being rejected by the rest of the group (Hazen, Black, & Fleming-Johnson, 1984).
- Be aware that even children who are able to play with others quite well will sometimes get stuck and need the help of an adult. This may be when the children have reached the end of a story they have been enacting or it may be when they have played a scene for quite some time. When play begins to fall apart, materials may be used inappropriately, scenes become repetitive, children wander out of the area, or the noise level increases. Before play reaches this point, offer a way to close the activity. Then suggest two or three new play themes they might act out.

Support Strategies

- Designate certain times of the day for small groups. Working in small groups can help children get to know each other. Make sure each child has opportunities to form relationships with others before changing group members.

> Tyrell and Shawn lived next door to each other and were friends at home as well as at child care. They preferred one another as playmates and even received comfort from each other when they were upset. On days that one of them was absent, the other tended to play alone rather than join the play of another child.
>
> Tyrell was at a loss when Shawn's family moved out of the city. For weeks he had difficulty playing with any other child at the center. His caregivers felt it was important to bring him together with others. To work on this, they invited Tyrell to join them as they played with the other children. They also paired him with children during art and table time. After a few weeks of such help making connections with others, Tyrell was able to play with a few of the other children. He still preferred to play with only one child at a time but now he had more children for play partners.

ENTRANCE TO A PLAY GROUP

When a child attempts to interact with other children or to join their play, he needs a number of strategies that will help him to be accepted by the group (Asher, Renshaw, & Hymel, 1982). There are two strategies that work best. In one, a child makes comments related to the established play, but the comments aren't directed toward anyone. In the second the child makes play-related comments directly to an individual. As he enters the group he must learn not to disrupt the play or to draw undue attention to himself (Hazen, Black, & Fleming-Johnson, 1984). Some children learn these strategies by watching others and some need more direct instruction as they learn to join a group.

Getting Ready to Enter a Group

In your care you may see children that stand outside the group and watch the activity but make no attempts to join the play. Other children may always choose toys that encourage solitary play. Before asking a child to join in group play, make sure the child feels competent in paired activities or in small group structured activities. If he is not, perhaps a goal regarding the child's level of interaction would be a good place to start. Use suggestions from the previous section before requiring him to join group play.

If a child is comfortable interacting with others in more structured settings but has difficulty joining ongoing play, he may have been rejected frequently and is no longer willing to try. If he stops trying he has no chance to improve his skills in this area.

Suggestions

During Play

- Facilitate opportunities for the child to join play by becoming a member of the group play. Once you are an active member of the play, invite this child to take on a role and join you.
- Place positive expectations that the child will join you later if he does not respond to your invitations right away. Say, "If you don't want to get on the bus right now, we'll stop for you next time around."
- Discuss confidentially what he would like to do in play. Suggest another child who likes to play the same thing and give him words to use to approach the other child. Suggest partners who are similar in development, temperament, and behavior as they are more likely to accept him (Rubin, 1980).

Support Strategies

- Tell stories about the benefits of being a group member (i.e., playing kick ball or having a tea party is more fun with a group than by yourself).
- Do a group puzzle. Create a large puzzle with a poster pasted on cardboard and cut up into as many pieces as you have children. Give each child a piece and then put the puzzle together. Emphasize how the group needs every person to make the puzzle whole.

Occasionally, force is used as a way to enter the group by children who have few other means of getting attention from group members. Some children rely on physical contact with others to initiate or enter play because they do not understand the more complex verbal strategies that are successfully used by others. Children who rely on physical contact to enter group play sometimes have difficulty changing strategies even when they find their first attempts are ineffective. Instead they repeat the same behavior, patting another child's back over and over or repeating a phrase like, "I want a turn. I want a turn." A child with more sophisticated skills would change strategies and try to negotiate a trade or talk about how they might use play materials together (Hazen, Black, & Fleming-Johnson, 1984).

Suggestions

During Play

- Interpret physical contacts a child makes for the other children. For example, when Jonathan arrived at the center, he called to the children from the car. He ran out to the playground at full speed and pushed Sam as he said, "You're it!" Sam turned and yelled, "Don't push me, Jon! You're not playing." A caregiver had been watching. She felt Jonathan had been trying to make contact with the rest of the children. She said to Sam, "I think Jonathan would like to play with you. Should he be 'it' or one of the runners?"
- In a confidential conversation with the child, let him know that the other children won't want to play with him if he hurts them. (Don't shame or embarrass him.) Tell him what to do instead of pushing. Jonathan, in the example above, could be told, "Sam didn't understand that you wanted to play. You could tell Sam, 'Hi Sam! I like to play tag too.' "
- Model the words he could use to join the play. In addition to the words modeled for Jonathan, you might suggest that he say, "I'm playing. I bet you can't catch me."
- Help this child to watch the play of others and to imitate some of their actions. This might be a successful strategy for many children as it is not dependent on words.

Support Strategies

- Use a developmental checklist to pinpoint the child's language skills. Are their skills age appropriate or lagging behind age expectations? Does this child need to have his skills assessed in more detail by a speech therapist?

Goal: Child will stand near the group and watch

Suggestions

During Play

- Before the child decides what he wants to do during a play session, walk with the child to a few areas where groups of children are playing and see what they are doing. Talk about their activities and what he might do if he were to join them.
- When you notice that the child is observing the play of others from where he sits or stands, invite him to walk closer to the group with you and watch for a while.
- Identify with the child which play group is appropriate for him to join. If a child wants to play firefighters, help him to look around the room to see what the other children are doing. Help him to decide which of the other activities is most related to his idea. Point out that it might be more appropriate for him to be a firefighter with a group of children playing with the blocks or in the housekeeping corner than with children who are playing with dinosaurs. If he attempts to join play too unrelated to his idea his attempt may be considered so disruptive he will be rejected.

Goal: Child will imitate behavior of group

Suggestions

During Play

- Become a parallel player and begin to imitate some of the actions of the others while on the fringes of the play. Encourage the child to do the same. Playing on the outskirts may give him some practice performing the actions and build his confidence level before he joins the group.
- Enter play by taking on a role that is related but not already taken. Be sure not to disrupt the existing play of the children. After you enter the play, invite the child who is watching to join you. In a scene about a restaurant you might pretend to be a customer, and then invite the child to come along.
- When the child is watching other children play, join him and discuss the activity of the group. Talk about the roles that he could take and how they fit into the ongoing play. For example, if there is a group of three playing in the housekeeping area and one is the mom, one the dad, and one the child, perhaps the newcomer could be the grandpa or the baby sitter. See if he can list some of the things that a grandpa would do in the setting.
- Make sure the roles you suggest are roles the child can enact. This helps to ensure success and increases the chance he will be willing to participate in the future. For instance, do not give a child with poor language skills a role that might require him to be highly verbal. He may set the tables at a restaurant rather than place the orders.

Goal: Child will make comments related to play

Suggestions

During Play

- Spend time playing with the child in paired activities. Set your play up near the play of other children. Watch for opportunities to join the play of the others and to bring this child with you. Perhaps you and he can play house near another group of children who are also playing house. Send him to their house to borrow some sugar for the cookies that you are making.
- Talk with the child about how he might fit into what the other children are doing. Model the words for him to use in joining the others. He might say, "We could build a garage for the cars with the blocks I have."
- Help the child make comments that correspond to the ongoing play. Question the child about what he is doing and how his play idea might fit with what the children are already doing. If he is unable to see how the ideas go together you may need to provide some help. For instance, he may want others to come to the store that he has set up while they are on a pretend camping trip. Help him to think about what someone who is camping may need to buy. Suggest that he sell batteries for flashlights and firewood for campfires.

Support Strategy

- Do a puppet play that shows a puppet trying to play with others. Show the strategies that he tries and the responses that he gets. End with the children brainstorming some things that the puppet could do to gain entry. Act the ideas out with the puppets.

Goal: Child will get the attention of another child before making comments related to play

Suggestions

During Play

- When a child tries to enter a group by making a comment, but his remarks are ignored, remind him to say the name of the other child. Model how to do this by repeating what was said but preface it with one of the children's names.
- Ask the child who he was talking to. Point out that you don't think the other child knew he was talking to him. Say, "I'm not sure Nathan knew you were talking to him. Say his name and when he looks at you tell him your idea again."

Support Strategies

- Teach all children to establish eye contact or call another child's name before beginning their conversations.
- Encourage children to call your name rather than tap your shoulder or tug your sleeve when they want your attention. Model the way to say, "Sheryl, could you help me?"

Michael Siluk

A WORD OF CAUTION

Asking "Can I play?" is considered to be the least effective of all entrance strategies, yet it is one that adults oftentimes suggest. Children who ask "Can I play?" too often hear the answer "NO!" (Hazen, Black, & Fleming-Johnson, 1984).

Children reject others for many different reasons. One reason may be to protect play materials. Another might be that they do not want to open their play to another child because they realize they will have to share materials with the newcomer.

Another reason is to protect the roles they have established. For instance, if two children are playing "service station" and one is the mechanic while the other is the owner of the broken motorcycle, they may not see a role for another child. In this case, the adult could point out that the newcomer could be the next customer or the cashier.

Children may also have difficulty seeing how to fit in one more player. In one such situation, Janet was setting the table for lunch. She had four chairs and four place settings for her guests. She set dolls at two of the place settings and invited Shelley to sit in one of the other chairs. Christopher was watching and the adult tried to draw him in to the play.

Adult: "Where is Christopher going to sit?"
Janet: "He can't come. There isn't any room. Two babies are in these chairs, one chair for Shelley and one chair for me."
Adult: "Maybe one of the babies could sit on Christopher's lap during lunch.
Janet: "Oh yeah! Christopher do you want to come for lunch?"

Janet had rejected Christopher simply because she saw no room for him!

The adult was able to find a simple way to make space for one more.

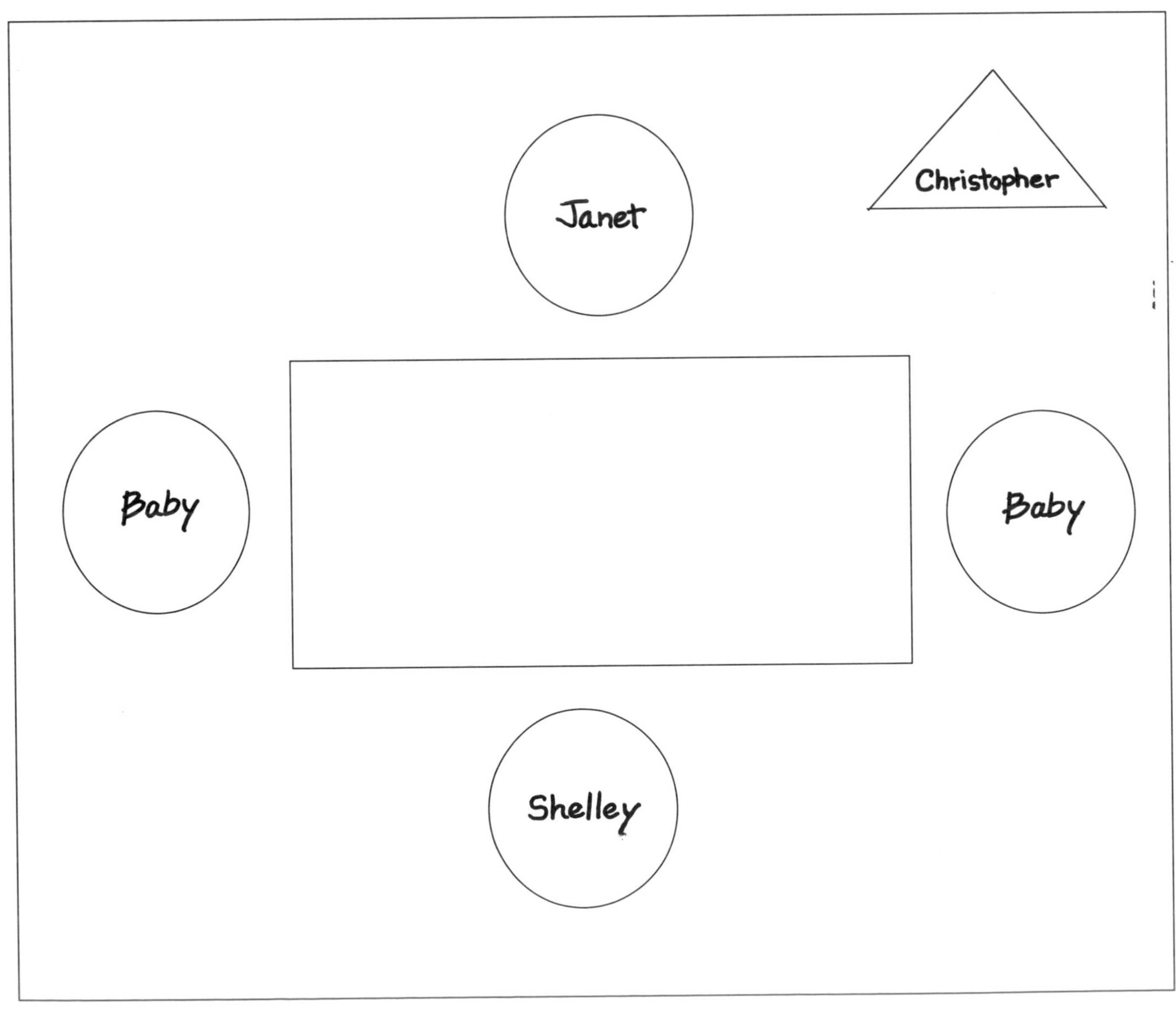

> Chad entered the block area saying, "We could play firefighters!" There was no response from any of the boys who were building a tall tower of blocks. Chad tried again saying, "Anybody want to play firefighters?" but still got no response from the others. Chad stood watching but was not invited to play.
>
> A few weeks later, Chad came into the housekeeping area where two children were pretending to set the table for breakfast. He carried a cup and said, "Here's your coffee." Chad continued to help with the imaginary breakfast preparations by cooking some bacon at the stove.
>
> This time Chad's attempt to enter was much more successful. He had learned to make his comments and actions relate to the ongoing play. In addition, his entrance did not take anything away from the existing play. Chad's comments would have had an even greater chance of drawing a favorable response if he had said "Brian, here's your coffee," or if he made sure that he had the attention of one of the other children before presenting his idea.

CONFLICT MANAGEMENT

Conflict is inevitable when young children come together. Unfortunately, some children try to resolve conflicts in aggressive ways. This makes them less likely to be accepted by the others in the group when they attempt to join in sociodramatic play (Asher, Renshaw & Hymel, 1982). Other children remain passive when someone tries to control them or their materials. The negotiation of these conflicts requires the skills of compromise and the ability to listen. Children must learn to resolve their disagreements in acceptable ways by describing their feelings, controlling aggressive impulses, and using words to take turns.

Getting Ready to Manage Conflict

Two inappropriate ways children respond to conflict include passivity and aggression. Before managing conflict by himself, the passive child must learn to stand up for himself and the aggressive child must learn to stop his actions before hurting someone. Toddlers sometimes don't know how to respond to others who take their toys or hurt them. They allow the other child to take their toy without any type of response. Some older preschoolers are similarly passive. If a child remains consistently passive when faced with conflict, he will not learn the skills of compromise and negotiation.

Suggestions

During Play

- Model words for the child to use in conflict situations such as "Mine!" or "Stop!" Even very young children can learn to use simple words such as these.
- Ask the child how he feels when another takes his toy. Ask him if that is ok with him. Help him to identify his feelings about the situation.
- Teach him to get an adult if he needs help in a conflict.

If a child uses force to solve conflicts, he must learn to stop his inappropriate behaviors. As he learns to stop one behavior, you must teach a behavior to replace it. For example, if a child learns to stop hitting in response to conflict, you must teach him to use words.

Suggestions

During Play

- Use the support strategies that follow to teach a child to stop and freeze. Then during play you can call his name when he is becoming upset but before he becomes aggressive. When he stops and freezes, you will have a few seconds to get to him and guide him through the situation.
- Stop the action in a conflict and have the children think of ways they might be able to solve the problem. In one family child care setting the caregiver used this technique very effectively. She had the children involved in the argument come and sit by her. She asked each child in turn what he thought the problem was. After they all had their turn to describe the situation, she asked, "How could you work it out so that everyone is happy?" The caregiver claimed that although it sometimes took a while, the children usually came up with their own solutions. The caregiver attributes the success of this technique to the opportunity it gives the children to calm down as well as to the problem-solving that the children do.
- Use the American Sign Language gesture for stop as you say the word, "stop." This gives the child a visual cue as well as a verbal direction. To sign "stop" extend your fingers on both hands. Place one hand out with the palm up. Use your other hand to cross your palm. The little finger side of this hand should be down.

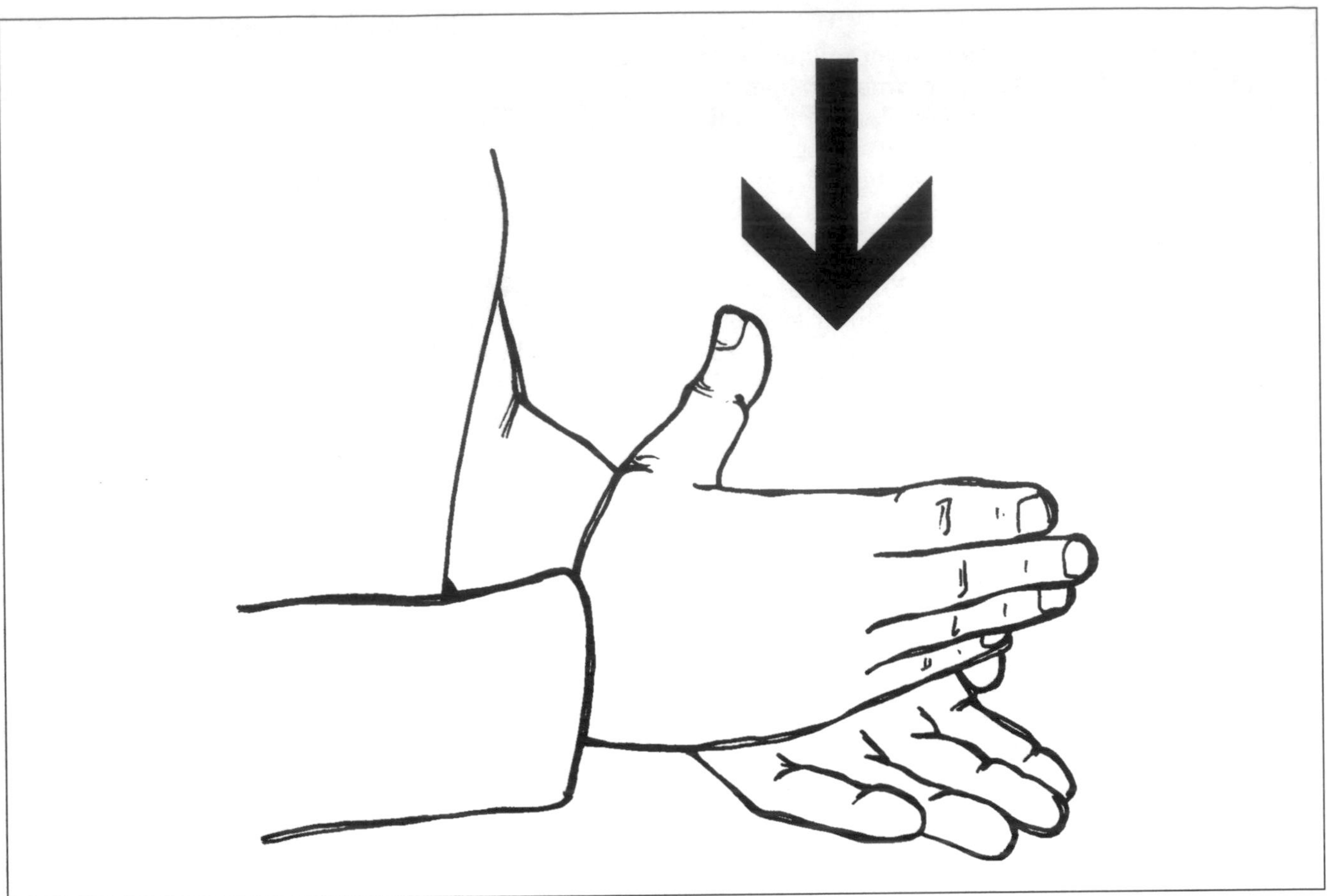

- Arrange associative play experiences for a time when sociodramatic play fails repeatedly on a given day. Set the children down side by side and have them play with similar materials such as Lego building blocks or Tinkertoys. This gives the players and you a break. You can try again later and may experience more success. Even children with complex play skills will occasionally find it difficult to play together.

Support Strategies

- Play lots of "stop-and-freeze" games with the children. In these games the child will learn to stop in response to an auditory cue such as a whistle, a drum, or a bell. Teach him to stop and freeze when you call his name, too. When he can do this successfully in game-like situations, have him practice stopping when you call his name in the middle of play time. Practice enough times so he can transfer this skill to a conflict situation.
- Teach the child to relax at various times throughout the day. Then when he is upset you can help him to relax using these techniques. Reaching a more relaxed state before trying to resolve the conflict can help everyone involved respond more calmly. For more ideas see Clare Cherry's book, *Think of Something Quiet* (1981).
- Build the child's vocabulary of words about feelings. Include words like frustrated, angry, scared, and many others. Elizabeth Crary's book *One Dozen Feeling Games* (1980) has many activities to help with this.
- Teach the child that there are different levels of intensity in emotion. For instance, you might teach the words irritated, angry, upset, *really* angry, and mad all to describe anger. When the child can use many words rather than just one he has more options for expressing his feelings.

Dealing with children who use force, especially those who are aggressive, is difficult for many caregivers. There are many good resource materials available that list techniques to use in teaching an aggressive child. A few that we have found helpful include: Clare Cherry's book, *Please Don't Sit on the Kids* (1983), Elizabeth Crary's books *Without Spanking or Spoiling* (1970) and *Kids Can Cooperate* (1984), and Eva Essa's book *A Practical Guide to Solving Preschool Behavior Problems* (1983).

In addition, you can help an aggressive child by teaching appropriate behavior. This helps you to be more positive in your approach and keeps your goals for the child focused on what he needs to learn. Goals that follow emphasize teaching the child to use words in conflict situations.

Goal: Child will ask adult for help

Asking for help in solving conflicts is actually a growth step for some children. If a child who has been aggressive in the past is left to solve a problem on his own, he may rely on the aggressive behaviors that he knows. For instance, if Jana wanted a turn on the swing a few months ago, she might have attempted to knock another child off. Now she has learned to ask an adult to help her ask for turns. By getting an adult, Jana gets help in learning more appropriate ways to ask for what she wants.

Some caregivers may become concerned because they feel that teaching a child to involve an adult will foster "tattling." Children tell adults about other's behavior for a few basic reasons:

- they are concerned that the child may cause injury to himself or others;
- they are scared by the child's actions;
- they need affirmation and approval for staying within the rules themselves; or
- they are trying to get the other child in trouble.

The last reason for telling is what is considered by many to be "tattling." You will need to use your professional judgement to determine when a child needs help with a situation, when he can be prompted to solve the problem on his own, and when he should be ignored (Katz, 1984). We believe that children who are just learning to solve conflicts need help from an adult. Later in this section we discuss ways to teach the child to be more responsible for solving the problem on his own.

Suggestions

During Play

- Encourage a child to ask for help when he begins to get frustrated.
- Go with the child to the area in which the problem is taking place and help to settle the problem.
- Talk for the children in a conflict situation. You might say to Jonathan, "Michael would like a turn with that." But if Jonathan isn't ready to give it up say, "It doesn't look like Jonathan is done yet." Say to Michael, "Let's watch to see when Jonathan leaves the dump truck and then it can be your turn. In the meantime there is a car you could play with."

Support Strategies

- Make asking for help acceptable in many situations by acknowledging that we all need help with certain things. Point out that you ask for help in getting the room cleaned up, Shelley asks for help when cutting things that have lots of corners and Jeremy likes help carrying the snack tray.

Learning to use words is the primary skill that the child needs in order to solve his conflicts appropriately. There appears to be a sequence in the way in which children learn to use words. The following chart helps to visualize what the adult does, the child's likely response, and the adult's reaction.

TO TEACH THE USE OF WORDS IN CONFLICTS

ADULT		CHILD		ADULT
provides the words	→	no response		
provides the words	→	imitates	→	praises each time
prompts the child to use words	→	recalls words used in the past	→	praises each time
		initiates the use of words	→	praises each time at first then praises on occasion

The next four sections discuss this sequence in further detail.

Goal: Child will imitate verbal solutions provided by the adult

A child may not know all of the phrases he could use in trying to resolve a conflict or to ask for a toy. He will need many opportunities to hear words that might help him get what he wants without resorting to force.

Suggestions

During Play

- Model the words for the child to use frequently. Tell him to say, "That's mine," or "I want that back," or "I've been waiting for a turn for a long time." The child will eventually begin to imitate the words that have been provided. Be sure to praise the child each time he repeats the words that you have given him.
- Remember that if you remove the toy or materials whenever there is a conflict, you remove the child's opportunity to learn more effective problem-solving skills. You may need to put things up for a short time, however, for your own sake.

Support Strategies

- Teach children to imitate by playing echo games. Clap a simple rhythm for the children to repeat. Play the game with many different rhythms and different leaders. You can also have the children play this game with simple phrases like "your nose is blue."

Goal: Child will recall words to use when reminded

Now the child should be ready to say the words he has been taught when you remind him.

We often expect children to come up with effective words on their own before they have heard appropriate words modeled by adults often enough. If a child is given the responsibility to "use words" before he is ready, the words he comes up with may be inappropriate. When Benjamin was told to "use words" he went back to the other child and said, "Get off my Big Wheel bike or I'll push you off."

Suggestions

During Play

- Prompt the child by reminding him to "use words." The child should go back to the situation and use words he recalls having been taught in the past.
- Make sure that the child's words work. This does not mean that he should always get his way but that the other children listen to him and respond. If Keisha had a toy first and she says to Sara, "Give it back, I had it first," it is important that Sara responds to the words Keisha uses either by giving the toy back or by working out a way to use it together.

Support Strategies

- Use a short puppet play to demonstrate how the children might resolve conflict over play material. First show the puppets fighting over whose turn it is and who gets to hold the blocks. Start the same scenario over again but this time stop when the puppets have difficulty sharing. Ask the children to suggest ways that they might solve the problem. Have the puppets act out the suggestions. Settle on the solution that seems to work best. Have the puppets act it out using the words that the children suggest. Go over the story again asking the children what took place and how the puppets worked out their problem. Let the children have opportunities to act out the story with the puppets. Repeat the puppet play using a similar story line but highlight other difficulties for the children to solve (Puppet Play Video, 1988).

WHEN TEACHING THROUGH PUPPETS

- introduce a short puppet story
- act out the story up to the point of the conflict
- ask the children how the puppets might solve the problem
- review the solutions
- let the children use the puppets to act out the story

Goal: Child will initiate use of words

Eventually, all of the teaching of appropriate words that you do will pay off. You will overhear a child using words on his own! Now he will no longer need to be told the exact words to use nor will he need reminders to use words.

Suggestions

During Play

- Recognize the child's appropriate behavior and comment to him about his growth in this area. Whisper to Susanna, "I heard you use your words to ask Ty for a turn. That used to be hard for you. You are learning to use words when you want a turn. Good for you."
- Help the child learn to wait for a turn or to cope with disappointment when he uses

words to ask for a turn and the answer is "NO!" Redirect him to another activity while he waits (Katz, 1984).

Goal: Child will accept reasonable compromises

Suggestions

During Play

- As conflicts arise in play, ask the children to brainstorm a number of solutions. Do not evaluate the solutions at this time. When a list of solutions has been developed, decide which ideas might work. Look at the consequences of each suggestion. Have the children decide which solution they will try out. Help them to get started (Crary, 1984).
- Make sure that children listen to the suggestions of others when they try problem solving on their own.

Support Strategies

- Read the book *Sam's Car* by Barbro Lindgren. In this book, Sam hits Lisa as she tries to take the car he is using. Ask the children how he might have solved the problem without hitting. Have them dictate their own ending to the story. They may also enjoy illustrating it.

> Shawn, a four-year-old boy, puffed out his chest, clenched his fist, and yelled in order to scare younger children into giving him a turn riding the Big Wheel bike. Unfortunately, Shawn's intimidation strategies worked and he was almost always successful at getting what he wanted.
>
> The adults working with this group of children decided that there were three parts to this problem. First, they agreed to teach the younger children to say no to Shawn when they were using a toy that he demanded. Second, they would help Shawn learn to use words when he asked for a turn. Finally, they were going to teach Shawn to find other things to do when he needed to wait for a turn. Their plan included many of the activities listed throughout this section.

TURN-TAKING

If there were a toy of each kind for every child, turn-taking would not be a skill children need. However, this is not the case and children must learn to share materials and adult attention to successfully play together. Successful turn-taking requires that they learn to give up toys when they have finished with them, participate in give and take situations, and learn to propose turn-taking. Successful turn-taking is essential to the sharing of props in sociodramatic play.

Brn Porter/Don Franklin

Getting Ready to Take Turns

When asked to share toys, some children will tantrum and clutch the toy to their chest. They may threaten others out of their arranged turns. They may always demand to be first in line. When a child is not able to take turns, set the stage for him to learn about sharing and turn-taking in everyday situations.

Suggestions

During Play

- Demonstrate sharing by being a generous role model yourself. When children experience generosity, they are more likely to be generous to others (Beaty, 1986).
- Set up dramatic play situations that give practice in turn-taking. Going to a bakery,

shoe store, restaurant, movie, and grocery store are examples of activities in which we must sometimes wait in line (Beaty, 1986).

Support Strategies

- Recognize times throughout the day when the child must wait for a turn, for instance, when it's time to use the bathroom or the drinking fountain. Comment on how well he is doing. Waiting in routine situations like these may be easier for some children than waiting for a toy. When they hear that they can be good at waiting for these turns they may also be encouraged to wait for turns in other types of situations.
- Practice giving to others by making simple gifts to exchange between the children in your group. One preschool periodically asks each child to bring an inexpensive Golden Book to give in a book exchange.

Goal: Child will leave a toy and not demand to have it back

Use this goal with a child who leaves a toy but protests if someone else picks it up.

Suggestions

During Play

- Make sure children have enough time with an object to feel as if they are done before asking them to give it up. Adults know from their own experiences that it is much easier to give up an object or activity they have had time to finish. This is true for children as well. Children are more likely to give up a material that they have had adequate time to explore and play with than something they just received (Beaty, 1986).
- Let a child feel in control when he passes on a toy. If, for some reason, you are unable to allow him to finish with it on his own, ask, "Are you going to give it to Tenisha in two minutes or in five minutes?"
- When a child is getting ready to leave a toy, remind him that if he leaves it other children will think he is done. Check to make sure that the child is really done. Say, "Are you all done with Mr. Potato Head? Then is it okay for Jessie to use it next?" Reinforce this idea at other times of the day, too. For instance, if the child leaves the snack table it means that he is done with snack. A problem might come up if a child won't risk leaving a toy long enough to use the bathroom. To avoid this you may need to make it clear that you will hold or protect a toy while the child uses the toilet.

Support Strategies

- Practice taking turns with the child. It may be easier for him to learn to take turns with an adult at first. Play a game that has a back and forth rhythm. Try bouncing or rolling a ball back-and-forth, or roll a car to each other. Return the toy right away so the child knows he will get it back if he really wants it.
- Don't expect children to share all materials. Identify with the child those objects that belong to him, such as his special blanket or cuddly toy. Identify those things that belong to other individuals. You might have a water glass or smock that belongs only to you. Be sure that you have special places to put those things which do not have to be shared. Then, if a child is not willing to share his private toy he can put it in this spot. However, keep in mind that some cultures encourage children to share everything; this value should be respected. The suggestion is meant for those children who truly need private spaces and materials.
- Take an inventory of all the toys in your setting with the child. Decide which objects belong to the group. Refer to these objects as the group's toys or the school's toys. You might say things like, "Let's take good care of the child care toys and get them all put away."

Goal: Child will willingly give up a toy if another child asks for it

This differs from the goal above because in this, the child is still using a toy when another child approaches him and asks for a turn. Many times a child will say, "Sure. I'm done anyway."

Suggestions

During Play

- If the child is sharing something of his own, reassure him that the toy will be returned. At first he may ask to have the toy back to check to see if the borrower is trustworthy (Davis, 1977).
- Encourage the child to tell the borrower how to use the toy if he is concerned about its safety. Teach the lender to say, "You can use it if you are careful," or "You can have a turn if you don't crash it into the wall" (Davis, 1977).

- Propose trades. No one likes to give up a material without something to take its place. Have the child who wants the toy think about something that the other child may want. He can take the new object to the child and suggest a trade (Katz, 1984).

Goal: Child will take turns that are arranged by an adult

Suggestions

During Play

- Teach a child to use words to ask for a turn in much the same way as described in the Conflict Management section (p. 69).
- Give the child waiting for a turn clues to look for so he can judge when it is his turn. For instance, he should watch to see when the other child puts the toy away because then he will know that he can have it. Or tell the child that it will be his turn to go down the slide when the child in front of him puts his feet on the ground.
- Help divide up the materials so that each child has some. Have the children practice dividing things, too.
- Draw the attention of children playing together to the arrival of a new child. Say, "Jamie wants to play but she doesn't have any playdough. Let's each give her a little of ours so that she has some." Some children may give only a pinch of dough while others give a little bigger chunk. Accept and thank the child for whatever portion he is willing to share.
- Talk the child through turn-taking. If needed, provide words for him to ask for a turn. Make sure that he gets a response even if the answer is "not right now." Help the child find out when it will be his turn. He can ask, "When will you be done?" or "Will you give it to me when you are done?" Be sure to watch so that the child playing with the toy doesn't forget who is next.
- Some caregivers use a timer to structure the length of time that each child has with popular pieces of equipment. Other providers object to this practice because it forces a child to give up an item even if he isn't done. We have found that many children begin to think about finishing their turn when given a warning that their time will soon be over. Then when the timer does go off, they are ready to give another child a turn.
- Make a "turn-taker." Cut a circle out of cardboard. Color one side red and the other side blue. When there is difficulty over who should have a toy, use the "turn-taker" to help to settle the dispute. Flip the "turn-taker" in the air. While it is in the air have one child guess which color will be showing. If he is right he is the first to use the toy (Davis, 1977).

Support Strategies

- Arrange times to practice turn-taking in fun situations. Tell the child you own the paper and he owns the crayons. Ask the child, "What could you do with your crayons? What could I do with my paper? If we shared with each other what could we do then?" (Davis, 1977).
- Try another paper and crayon activity. Give the child a piece of paper. You take a crayon. Tell him the crayon cannot be divided into two pieces. Ask, "We both want to draw, how can we do it?" (Davis, 1977).

Goal: Child will ask for a turn and wait for a response.

Suggestions

During Play

- Check the rhythm of the turn-taking. Remember that there must be a pause between asking for a toy and taking it. The pause allows the other child the opportunity to respond.
- Remind the child asking for a turn to wait for the other child to give the toy to him. One time Cassy was leaning her doll on a stack of towels as she dressed her. Kelly came by and asked to use a towel and at the same time tried to take one off the pile. It happened so fast that Cassy and her doll were nearly knocked over. The adult tried to steady Cassy and said, "Give her a chance, Kelly. I'm sure she'll give you a towel."

Goal: Child suggests a sequence of turns

This refers to a sequence of turns with a toy or material, as well as with play ideas. Many four and five year olds will spend time arguing about what to play. Often they learn that they must give and take with their play ideas as well as they give and take with toys.

Suggestions

During Play

- Reinforce the child for proposing turn-taking. Point out his growth in this area. Marcia's ability to arrange turns was praised by her caregiver when she said, "I'm glad you think about ways that you and Rachel both get a chance to use the steering wheel. You are really learning to take turns."

Support Strategy

- Ask the children to establish the rules for using a new toy or material. Have them think about how many people can use it and for how long (Beaty, 1986).

> Mollie had been setting the table with the toy dishes. A few minutes later, she went on to dress her doll. LaToya entered the housekeeping area and began to collect the dishes. All of a sudden Mollie came running from across the room. She took the dishes out of LaToya's hands and said, "You can't have these. I'm playing with them." Mollie had not used the dishes for some time. But from her outburst it was apparent that she was not done with them. LaToya had no way of knowing this and was quite surprised when Mollie appeared.
>
> To help Mollie learn that when she left a toy others would think she was done, Mollie's caregiver started watching more carefully to see when she left a toy. She checked with Mollie to see if she really was done. She reminded Mollie that if she played somewhere else she couldn't expect things would stay exactly as she left them. Sometimes with this type of reminder, Mollie decided to stay and play with the toys a while longer. Other times Mollie didn't seem to mind. In addition, Mollie's caregiver reminded the children at snack that when they left the table it meant that they were finished. Soon Mollie learned she couldn't control materials she was not using.

SUPPORT OF PEERS

The relationships that children build with one another in child care settings can be very positive. Children who are in full-time child care can develop friendships that sometimes resemble or improve upon the relationships of siblings. Children provide one another with friendship and companionship and can even offer a sense of security to one another in stressful situations (Rubin, 1980). To be successful in developing and maintaining relationships with others, children must learn to be supportive of their peers.

The goals in this section represent a group of skills which are essential in developing positive, accepting friendships. Attending to others, offering comfort or help when someone is distressed, sharing power and leadership in play, and showing approval are ways in which children demonstrate the friendship skills which make up this section (Asher, Renshaw, & Hymel, 1982). Without these skills, a child may not be allowed to be a member of the group during sociodramatic play.

Goal: Child will watch peers

Some children do not look at or show interest in others in the group. Consequently, they don't notice facial expressions and body posture that give clues as to how others are feeling.

Suggestions

During Play

- Prompt the child to look at you while you talk. You can do this by putting your hand under his chin and gently raising his head while at the same time verbally reminding the child to look at you. If the child has difficulty establishing eye contact, suggest that he look at your face or at your mouth as you speak. Caution: Among some cultures eye-to-eye contact is considered disrespectful. If the child is resisting, do not force him.

Support Strategies

- Ask the child to look at the faces of the people in the books that you read with him. Ask the child what he thinks each person might be feeling. How can he tell?
- Label other people's feelings as you notice them. If you are out on a walk and you notice people laughing or singing, talk about what they might be feeling and what clues lead you to believe they are happy or sad.
- Be sure that the child knows feeling words. Teach a variety of words to describe a variety of emotions.
- Find pictures from magazines that show people expressing various emotions. Ask the child to act out some of the feelings that the people in the pictures are showing. Ask the child:

  What is happening in the picture?
  How is the person feeling? How can you tell?
  What will the person do now?
  What can we do to make her feel better?

Adapted from Burton and Woltag, 1986.

Bm Porter/Don Franklin

Goal: Child will offer help

A part of supporting others is to offer help when someone is sad, frustrated, or can't manage on his own.

Suggestions

During Play

- When a child watches another child who is crying, suggest that he take the crying child a toy or give her a hug. A child may be able to sympathize with the child who is crying but be unaware of how to help. One day Vincent watched intently as Jessica cried. As he watched his bottom lip began to quiver. The caregiver suggested that Vincent take Jessica a doll she enjoyed holding. Vincent's "sympathetic crying" suggests that he was beginning to understand how others feel.

Support Strategies

- Discuss what the children would do if they heard a baby crying; if they were crossing the street and heard a horn honk; if they were walking by a barking dog. Talk with the children about how sounds help them know how to behave (Burton and Woltag, 1986).
- Play sound identification games with a tape recorder to draw the children's attention to auditory cues, especially those that indicate someone needs help. Tape common sounds like running water, a siren, a baby crying, or someone laughing. Play the tape back and have the children guess what the noises are.
- Find magazine pictures of people who look sad. Have the children role play different ways to make the "sad" person happy, such as a hugging, holding hands, or inviting the person to play (Burton and Woltag, 1986).
- Role-play with the children ways they can help if someone:

  spills milk or water
  drops a cup of beans
  spills sand out of the sand box
  knocks over the block tower that someone is building

Burton and Woltag, 1986.

- Set up dramatic play areas that encourage the children to act out caring for others. You might read the book *Sam Who Never Forgets* (1977) and then arrange a zoo in the block area. Let the children take turns caring for the animals as Sam does in the book. Or set up a veterinarian's office. Use stuffed animals as the animals that visit the veterinarian. Visit the Humane Society or ask a veterinarian to talk with your group.
- Talk with the children about when someone they knew was sick. Ask them about the special kinds of care the sick person needed or about things that people did to help the sick person to feel better. Try to develop a lengthy list of things that they can do to help. Include:

  get special toys for them
  make them foods that won't upset their stomach
  turn the channel on the t.v.
  bring something for them to do
  talk quietly while they are napping
  draw a picture for them to look at

Burton and Woltag, 1986.

- Act out caring for sick people in the housekeeping area (Burton and Woltag, 1986).

Goal: a) Child offers suggestions to ensure the continuation of play
b) Child accepts play suggestions of others

These goals refer to turn-taking in a social sense. Here children take turns with ideas and leadership rather than materials. If a child does not offer suggestions, he may be allowed to play and may even be sought out as a playmate. But as a passive player, he never learns what his creative potential could be. On the other hand, if a child never accepts the play suggestions of others, he will be bossy and controlling. In many cases, this leads to a clash among players. A child who cannot accept the suggestions of others may be excluded.

If a child is unable to do either you will want to choose one of the two goals listed here. Try the suggestions listed here as well as those under the item "accepts reasonable compromises" in the Conflict Management section (p. 69) and "suggests a sequence of turns" in Turn-taking (p. 73).

WORD OF CAUTION

It's not always in a child's best interests to take the suggestions of others. Whether or not a child should take the suggestions of others needs to be judged each time it occurs. Sometimes children may make suggestions that are inappropriate. Furthermore, a child may succumb to the wishes of others so often that he no longer asserts himself. There should be a balance between accepting suggestions and offering them.

Suggestions

During Play

- (a and b) Praise all the children for having good ideas. Emphasize that *many* children in the group have good ideas. Elicit lots of differing thoughts about the way that play could go. Ask the children, "Whose idea should we play first?"

  After play has been directed by one child for a time or when play gets stuck and you need a new idea:

  a) talk with the child about his play idea. If necessary, ask questions that allow him to choose like, "do you think we should take the babies shopping or to the ice cream store?"

  b) talk with the child about trying someone else's idea.

- (b) Confidentially talk with the child about how his unwillingness to play other people's ideas might discourage them from playing with him. Tell him, "Your friends might not want to play if they don't get a chance to play their ideas." Emphasize what he can do differently so the others will play with him by saying, "But if you try out Jana's idea about the spaceship she might play with you a while longer."

- (b) Point out the importance of all the roles assigned to children in a play scenario. Make less prominent roles more acceptable by adding costumes or giving them a special task. For instance, the role of the family dog can be enhanced by adding a tail or suggesting that he get the slippers and perform tricks.

Support Strategies

- (a and b) Encourage the children to build on one another's story lines by drawing group pictures and telling group stories. To make a group picture, one child starts the picture by drawing one part, then passes the picture on to another child who adds another part.

- (a and b) Use puppet play as described in the section Verbalizations about Play Scenario (p. 55) to encourage turn-taking about play ideas.

Goal: Child will encourage and praise others during play

Children who do well socially are able to praise their peers. They say things like, "That's a nice tower," and "Good job," or "You look pretty" (Asher, Renshaw, & Hymel, 1982).

Suggestions

During Play

- Praise the child often. Comment on things he does well and things that he has learned. This offers a model of how to praise others.

- Encourage the child to praise himself. Start by saying, "I really like the way you built your tower so high. What do you like about it?" It is important for a child to feel good about himself before expecting him to be able to feel good about others and to praise them.

- Have the child tell another child when he notices something special. Oftentimes when a child notices something nice about his friend he tells an adult about it. Megan might say, "Did you see Rachel's pretty picture?" Help Megan to praise Rachel by encouraging her to tell Rachel that she likes her picture.

- Turn negative conversations about another child into positive ones. If a child comments about Mark's scribbling, help the child think of all of the things that Mark does really well. For instance, Mark might be using a nice combination of colors, staying on the paper with his crayons, or working hard at getting the whole figure covered up with color. By turning the conversation around you set the tone for a more positive discussion and demonstrate to the child that you will not talk negatively about a child's abilities.

Support Strategy

- Schedule a time each day when children practice saying something nice to one another. One caregiver did this as part of her lunchtime conversation. Each child at the table said at least one nice thing about the child sitting next to him. At first the comments were about the "pretty blue dress" or the "neat suspenders." After some practice the children were able to talk about things they saw another child do that morning. One child said "I really liked the garage you were building today. I wish I could have played with you." For more ideas on helping children to praise one another refer to a kit called "Very Important Kid" (1989). This kit offers materials that focus on building self-esteem. Each child becomes the "Very Important Kid" for a week. The other children in the group give compliments and praise to this child.

Marie hit Lexi. Both Marie and Lexi were upset about the situation and started crying. Marie was asked to sit down for a short time while the caregiver focused on comforting Lexi. Soon Lexi felt better but was concerned because Marie was still crying. She asked the caregiver, "Is she just going to keep on crying all day?" The caregiver asked Lexi what she might do to help Marie feel better. Lexi thought that Marie might stop crying if she had her blanket. Lexi offered the blanket to Marie and she took it gratefully. When things calmed down, the caregiver talked with the girls about how they might be able to resolve the situation that had caused them both to become so upset.

TIME FOR ACTION

We have given you many ideas to try. Continue your planning process by designing lessons that will appeal to you and your child. Next comes the most rewarding part of your careful work. Try the lessons for an extended period of time. You should see a child learning play skills that will enrich and expand his play experience. You can feel proud of your part in that growth.

CHAPTER 7

PUTTING IT ALL TOGETHER

In this chapter, we come to the final step: putting it all together. It is time to step back, observe what you have done, and evaluate how your child reacted. Evaluation is an important part of the process at the time of the lesson and, after months of work, as you measure progress towards your goal. In reality however, evaluation is not the final step. Evaluation is only the next step that leads again to another plan of action. The important role that evaluation plays is illustrated in the following case study and discussion. In this chapter we discuss:

Lori: A Case Study
The Value of Evaluation
Final Thoughts

LORI: A CASE STUDY

Lori was a three-year-old child with a very short attention span and limited play skills. She was old enough to move into the three-year-old class but couldn't because she couldn't participate in group activities. She flitted from activity to activity without a look backward. Adult attempts to help Lori focus or extend her attention resulted in little improvement. She only did minimal pretend play sequences. Terry, her teacher, knew there were family circumstances that greatly influenced Lori's behavior. Lori's mother had lived with a man who had often beat her since Lori was born. Lori's baby sister had already been removed from the home because of physical abuse. However difficult the family circumstances, the fact remained that Lori couldn't move into the next class until her skills improved. Terry knew that she couldn't control what happened at home for Lori, but she could focus on Lori's behavior at school.

Michael Siluk

After Terry had observed Lori, Terry did the Play Checklist. The areas that Lori had difficulty with were:

Persistence in Play	Conflict Management
Interactions	Turn-taking

Terry chose a goal on persisting in play. She felt that many of the other skills could be worked on when Lori was able to stick with a chosen activity. She felt that play would be an excellent way to engage Lori's interest.

Through her observations, Terry had been able to complete the checklist. She also learned several things about Lori. She learned that Lori rarely stayed with a play activity beyond one or two minutes. She saw that Lori might stay longer with an adult but if the adult's attention was diverted for any reason, Lori ran off. Lori would play a little longer if she was doing a sensorimotor activity. Lori would often push adults and children away by swearing, calling names, or having tantrums. These behaviors tended to happen when Lori was in a group of children. Terry's observations gave her important clues about how best to help Lori improve her play skills.

Plan 1

Following is the first lesson plan that Terry did with Lori:

PLANNING FORM

Child's Name: *Lori*

GOAL

Who: *Lori*

Does What: *will persist in play with an adult*

How well or how often: *for five minutes*

Target Completion Date for Goal: *5/29/92*

LESSON PLAN

Date: *2/12/92*

When will you work on the lesson? *free play*

What are the child's special interests? *sensorimotor activities*

How many children will be involved? *Lori*

Where will the playing take place? *preschool classroom*

What props will be needed? *dolls, lotion for soap, water, dish pan, wash cloths, towels*

Your role: *play tutoring — inside role*

Activities during play: *washing babies, drying babies, putting lotion on babies*

Support Strategies: *none at this time*

Terry used a sensorimotor activity, water play, with a dramatic play theme, washing babies. She predicted that this would help Lori stay involved. Because Lori would often run away when an adult's attention was divided, Terry included only herself and Lori in the activity. In order to do this, Terry had to plan with other staff how this activity would fit in the class routines. This joint planning ensured the plan would be supported by other staff members.

Evaluation

After Terry had done the activity, she was able to proudly report that Lori had played for thirty minutes with babies. She had wandered off two times but Terry was able to lure her back with the towels to dry the babies. In regular classroom play, Lori would rarely come back even when an adult would call her.

Besides the obvious increase in Lori's attention span, Terry noted that Lori was able to be quite gentle with the baby as she imitated Terry's actions. She washed the different parts of the body and labeled the neck, fingers, legs and other body parts as Terry did. Terry was surprised that Lori's attention lasted so long, especially the first time. It often takes longer to see such dramatic results. Terry felt the success of this lesson plan was due in part to her observation and use of Lori's play preferences. Terry knew she was on the right track. She decided to plan two more play themes that combined sensorimotor activities and dramatic play.

Plan 2

The following is the second lesson plan.

PLANNING FORM

Child's Name: *Lori*

GOAL

Who: *Lori*

Does What: *will persist in play with an adult*

How well or how often: *for five minutes*

Target Completion Date for Goal: *5/29/92*

LESSON PLAN

Date: *2/19/92*

When will you work on the lesson? *on a home visit*

What are the child's special interests? *sensorimotor activities*

How many children will be involved? *Terry and Lori with mother joining*

Where will the playing take place? *In the home*

What props will be needed? *pans, dishes, spoons, salt and pepper shakers, doll, bottle, and dried beans*

Your role: *play tutoring — inside role*

Activities during play: *pretending to cook and feeding baby*

Support Strategies: *none at this time*

Evaluation:

Terry again saw a dramatic increase in Lori's attention span. She played for twenty minutes and only left the activity once. She came back easily. She performed many of the actions of cooking and feeding: stirring, seasoning, smelling, dishing out, and feeding the doll and her mother. At home with fewer distractions, she was able to better concentrate. Toward the end of the activity, Lori pretended to cook less and did more of the sensorimotor activity, pouring. An unexpected benefit to this activity was the involvement of her mother. Lori pulled her mother into the play in an easy and nonthreatening way.

Terry planned another play activity to reinforce the learning that was occurring.

Plan 3

This is the third lesson plan.

PLANNING FORM

Child's Name: *Lori*

GOAL

Who: *Lori*

Does What: *will persist in play with an adult*

How well or how often: *for five minutes*

Target Completion Date for Goal: *5/29/92*

LESSON PLAN

Date: *3/5/92*

When will you work on the lesson? *free play*

What are the child's special interests? *sensorimotor activities*

How many children will be involved? *Lori*

Where will the playing take place? *in the classroom*

What props will be needed? *sand, tub for sand, cars and trucks, a small grader to build roads*

Your role: *play tutoring — inside role*

Activities during play: *building roads in the sand*

Support Strategies: *praise Lori when she stays with an activity throughout the school day*

Evaluation

Although Lori did play for ten minutes building roads, she didn't play as long as in the first two lessons. After some thought, Terry felt this was because Lori knew more about cooking and washing babies than about building roads. She also may have been more interested in babies and cooking. Yet Terry noted that Lori did stay involved longer than the two minutes she had observed initially.

To test whether combining sensorimotor play and dramatic play truly helped Lori persist, Terry planned an activity in the classroom for herself and Lori. If it was just an adult's presence that helped Lori concentrate, Lori would play a similar length of time with any activity that involved an adult's support. She brought out bristle blocks and sat with Lori to play with them. Lori only sat there for two minutes and ignored Terry's requests to come back. By this small experiment Terry knew that Lori not only needed an adult to expand her attention span, but also activities that combined dramatic play and sensorimotor play. Terry's lesson plans did work to help Lori stay with a play activity.

Where to go next?

Terry planned eight more lessons that addressed her original goal. When the target completion date arrived, she sensed that she had reached her goal. To be sure, she observed Lori during free play. Lori could play with an adult for five minutes.

Terry had found a formula that worked for Lori. When Lori stayed with the dramatic play, she was able to extend and expand on the theme. Her behavior was more positive. There were no tantrums, less name calling, and less swearing. Lori felt successful and her self-esteem was enhanced. All these were positive benefits.

But Terry knew the next step would be to include other children in the play. Terry felt that it would be most helpful to begin with just one child and proceeded to plan play experiences that would accommodate more children.

A year later when Lori was three and a half years old, she was able to persist in play for ten minutes, especially if it was something she liked to do with other children. Terry's concentration on Lori's play had paid off as Lori matured. She still had difficulties with conflict management and her teachers continued to work on these goals in Lori's play. But their involvement was not as close or extensive. Lori was beginning to solve conflicts on her own.

THE VALUE OF EVALUATION

From the case study, you can see that Terry used her evaluation of the lesson plans in many ways. Terry knew that her plan to combine sensorimotor play and dramatic play did increase Lori's attention span. She learned that Lori spent more time with dramatic play themes that Lori knew and understood. Terry knew when she was ready to include other children in her plan.

From Terry's experience, we can see that evaluation is an important step in the process. Listed below are reasons that evaluation is so vital:

- Evaluation helps you decide when your lesson plan did not accomplish its purpose.
- Evaluation points you to your next lesson plan.
- Evaluation at the time of the target completion date helps you decide if you have met your goal.
- Evaluation gives you information for your next goal.

Sometimes, caregivers only do one lesson plan and then lose focus on the play goal. This means children do not receive reinforcement for the progress they have made, nor do they have a chance to extend their learning. Think of your involvement in a child's play as more than a one-time plan. For most children who are having difficulty, you have to continue your involvement. The chart below illustrates the steps.

1. Observe
2. Do the Play Checklist
3. Decide on a goal
4. Plan a lesson
5. Implement the lesson
6. Observe and evaluate the lesson
7. Repeat steps 4, 5, & 6 frequently before the target completion date
8. On the target completion date observe to check progress toward goal
9. Write new goals
10. Recycle to step 4

As you recycle through this process you will help the child continue her learning throughout the year.

FINAL THOUGHTS

As we have written this book, we have focused on each step in a rather orderly fashion. We are acutely aware that life rarely progresses in such a fashion and children's growth probably never does. We know that as you try the ideas in this book, you may experience discouragements. The decisions and plans you make as a caregiver may not work as quickly as you wish. You may intuitively do something that works and yet your carefully laid plans may fizzle. You may see immediate progress and then there will be a plateau in growth. You may not see all the progress while the child is in your care. The skills may not become natural to her until she matures. These are variables that we expect and even welcome. Each child's growth is individual and unique.

Despite the element of the unexpected in children's learning, we have outlined the steps of teaching play skills concretely and in a certain order. In our experience, the order has made our work with children more consistent and more helpful, especially to the child who is having trouble. After plans have been laid, the actual play with the child becomes spontaneous and alive.

When a child learns to play more cooperatively both you and the child will gain. You will be able to observe and enjoy the unfolding of enriched and positive play instead of policing destructive play. You will be more aware of how the child is changing and growing because you have been an important part of that growth. Because you have learned about play and its components, you will be able to help parents understand their child's progress with play skills.

While the child is in your care, she will increase her positive self-esteem and confidence because she is more successful in play. She may elaborate the roles she plays with greater accuracy. She may better fit into a play group. She may more easily resolve her conflicts, may communicate her ideas with more fluency, and may show empathy towards her friends. She may even practice leadership skills as she puts forth new play ideas. As we enumerate the tremendous learning that can take place in play, we see the lessons extend far beyond childhood. Being able to think imaginatively, resolve conflict with grace, trade ideas with others and be compassionate are the building blocks for human relationships. As you read this book you may wonder with us how different some adult lives would be if they had learned these play skills as children.

Bm Porter/Don Franklin

APPENDIX 1

CHILDREN WHO HAVE DIFFICULTY LEARNING PLAY SKILLS

As we have discussed children who have difficulty learning play skills, you may have thought of several children in your care who aren't playing with other children. They may look very unhappy, may pick fights every time they come near a group of children, or may just simply avoid all contact. Through the weeks of observation, these behaviors hold consistent.

The question, "Why can't they play with other children?" may come to your mind. Although the answer to this question is not needed to effectively help, there are several factors that may interfere with a child's developing ability to play with others. Many of these factors are outside your control. Despite this you can help a child become successful in play in your setting. The seriousness of these factors range from the easy-to-fix to the very difficult. Following is a list of some of the factors that can interfere with a child's ability to play with others:

- Shyness
- Lack of Experience
- Unusual Play Themes
- Emotional Traumas
- Abuse and Neglect
- Language Difficulties
- Cognitive Delays

The first three variables we discuss are less complex. Often children with these problems can be helped more quickly and with less of your direct involvement than children with the more chronic difficulties in the next four variables. Children with chronic difficulties can present an overwhelming picture. Caregivers may not be able to decide what they can do about any of the problems. Since you cannot control other factors such as home environment or developmental delays, it is most helpful to focus on behaviors that you see in your setting. Regardless of the difficulties the child may encounter, you can help the child gain better sociodramatic play skills.

SHYNESS

Some children may be temperamentally shy from birth on. Shy children will be onlookers for a much longer time than other children. They often become very quiet around groups. However, parents may report that at home the children are lively and talkative. Although their behavior can look quite withdrawn, they tend to move quickly when you try techniques outlined in this book.

LACK OF EXPERIENCE

Children may simply be unexposed to dramatic play. When it is time to pretend, they don't know how to join in. Sometimes this lack of exposure is to a particular play theme, such as office play or riding in an airplane. Other times, children may not have received much stimulation or encouragement to play in their home. If you suspect that the children need more experience, you can provide field trips, modeling, and books to encourage play.

UNUSUAL PLAY THEMES

Some children may devise unusual and imaginative play themes that are unfamiliar to the other children. Often these children are ignored because the rest of the group does not know how to play along. You can provide a bridge for the children by explaining the different parts they can play or by providing a model to imitate. It is important to support the children who think up new play themes as this shows great imagination and creativity. Playing these themes may result in a fun adventure for your whole group.

EMOTIONAL TRAUMAS

Any trauma, whether death of a parent or loved one, divorce, or chemical abuse in the family, can result in a diminished ability to play. The loss of self-esteem, control, and overwhelming feelings impair a child's ability to open himself to new experiences and other people. This may occur for only a short time or can stretch throughout childhood.

ABUSE AND NEGLECT

Abuse in the home can affect both the child's developmental level of play and the amount of participation in play (Howard, 1986). Children who experience violence in the home may be less likely to engage in fantasy (Freyberg, 1973). Some of the play behaviors you may see with an abused or neglected child are:

Bizarre play themes that are violent or strange in nature. For example, a child may use small people for food or beat up dolls excessively. These behaviors may drive other children away rather than bring them in.

Behavior difficulties in the context of play, such as hitting, poor impulse control, or little frustration tolerance.

Reduced ability to carry on pretend themes or use objects to pretend. Delayed language or cognitive abilities as a result of the abuse and neglect may slow down a child's acquisition of representational skills.

Heightened anxiety around certain play themes or areas. For example, if the child has been abused in the kitchen, the house corner may be only a reminder of that pain.

Blanking out during play. When the child comes out of a trance-like state, the play has moved on and it is difficult to re-enter.

The child may have little flexibility in conflict resolution and an impaired ability to empathize with others.

LANGUAGE DIFFICULTIES

If a child has difficulty expressing thoughts and feelings, it is hard to enter or participate in play. Some verbal substitutions may be impossible to express even if the child knows what he wants to say. A child with language delays may withdraw from all contact. Others may express their frustration in aggression and tantrums.

COGNITIVE DELAYS

Cognitive delays can affect the quality and amount of play a child does. Some studies have suggested that children with special needs may go through the same developmental sequence, as other children, only more slowly (Heidemann, 1981; Lederlein, 1987). This would also affect their play developmental levels. Some children with severe mental retardation or autism may have rigid play behaviors that limit how much symbolic play they do (Wing, Gould, Yeates, & Brierly, 1977).

This slower development and/or rigid play sequences can isolate a child with cognitive delays from the other children. Only with adult modeling or interaction with other children can associative or cooperative play develop (Lederlein, 1987).

As the list suggests, some children who have difficulty with play in groups also can have delays in other areas. If you notice that a child is consistently left behind or not joining in, it is essential that you look at other areas of development: language, cognitive, emotional, and motor. If you believe you observe such a delay, and if the child is not already receiving special services, refer the child. *However, your involvement does not end with that referral.* You can still help that child learn to play more successfully in your environment by using the suggestions included in the book.

APPENDIX 2

INFORMATION FOR TRAINERS

This appendix gives ideas and suggestions for those of you who would like to share the information in this book with other caregivers.

"I didn't realize how complex play is."

"This has helped me to focus on the things children can learn during play."

"The workshop got me interested in playing with the children again. I had been so busy with other things I forgot how important play can be."

These are some of the comments we have heard from people attending workshops and classes where the information contained in this book was presented.

Unfortunately, caregivers don't always realize the value of play and their involvement in it. Too often they use the time that children are "just playing" to do many of the other tasks that are required of them. While these tasks are important, it is essential that the caregiver be involved in play and available to facilitate learning if play is to offer an optimal growth opportunity. By learning more about play, many caregivers develop an understanding of the importance of play. They also gain an interest in the possibilities of play. Caregivers have told us they feel rejuvenated and ready to engage in play after attending one of the workshops.

This information will provide people educating caregivers with:

Activity Ideas
Difficulties
Enhancers

ACTIVITY IDEAS

People educating adults must recognize the vast knowledge and experience that the participants bring with them to educational settings. Facilitating activities so they can share with one another becomes one of the goals of adult education. At the same time we have found that some of the people currently caring for children in child care settings lack basic information about the development of play and social skills. Maintaining a balance between a formal presentation of information and a free exchange of ideas among caregivers is important in developing an interesting and participatory workshop. We have found that a rhythm that works best for us is one in which we present material in lecturettes lasting no longer than twenty to thirty minutes followed by a time for people to process the information and share with one another in a related activity.

In addition we have found that the material is quite easy for caregivers to accept when presented in a logical sequence. People come away from the lecturettes thinking that the information is easy to understand. It is not until they try to apply the information in their settings that they find there is much more to it than there first appears. Using activities and case studies helps people to use the information in the workshop setting. Questions can be asked and discussion usually follows.

Some activities are described below.

The Opening Activity

To set an atmosphere of sharing and to get people to begin thinking about play, we open each training with a play activity. Small groups are given a number of props. The props are made up of recognizable toys as well as unidentified objects. These might include:

- a soccer shin pad, old radio speakers, a pastry wheel, and a tea bag squeezer
- Weeble People
- small cubes
- ceramic tiles with pictures on them
- paper, markers, tape, paper punch, and stapler

The groups are asked to play with the materials and note *how* they play as well as *what* they do with the objects. About halfway through the exercise people are told they can trade objects with other groups as long as the entire group agrees to the trade.

The comments made by the group members are usually very interesting and can be used to illustrate points throughout the course of the workshop. For instance, in one session the group used the

Weeble People to tell the story of *Goldilocks and the Three Bears*. This was used as an example of representation and dramatic play skills. The techniques used by the participants to negotiate trades parallel those used by children. Using quotes from those involved in the exercise to talk about negotiation skills makes the concepts presented more understandable.

Ice Breakers

Ice breakers are short exercises that help to build trust among group members and establish an atmosphere of sharing. They help participants to make informal contacts with others and get started talking with one another. Ice breakers are usually the best when they relate to the material you will be discussing and get people to begin thinking about the topic at hand. For one ice breaker, you may want to pair participants and have them describe their observations of a child in their setting. They can then show where they plotted the child's skills on the Play Checklist. Another ice breaker may be a large group brainstorm of the materials available in child care settings that promote sociodramatic play. Be creative in developing your own ice breakers and in finding ways to link people to one another. For more ideas see the books *Games Trainers Play* (1980) and *More Games Trainers Play* (1983) by Scannell and Newstrom.

Videotape Excerpts

As we developed the material for classes, we put together a videotape of children demonstrating some of the skills listed in the Play Checklist. This has proven again and again to be a valuable tool in discussing the skills that children need to be successful in sociodramatic play. The videotape focuses on the behaviors described in the Play Checklist. Participants watch the children and then decide what level of play the children are demonstrating. For example, in a scene where children are trying to solve a conflict, the participants are asked to decide if the children are able to initiate the use of words, recall words to use when reminded, or to imitate verbal solutions provided by the adult. This gives people an opportunity to clarify any misperceptions before they complete the checklist on their own.

A videotape of a caregiver using some of the techniques discussed in the chapter on Your Role was also developed.

If you are unable to develop a videotape specifically for this purpose, it is likely that videos already available (especially those on observation, dramatic play, or unedited footage of children engaged in dramatic play) would provide you with a number of rich examples from which to pull.

Case Studies

Case studies have been used to help workshop participants understand the information that is presented. Working through the process with a case study allows caregivers a chance to discuss how they might choose from a number of possible goals the ones that they would prioritize for an individual.

Divide participants into small groups and ask each group to write a goal for the child presented in the case study and then list activities that might be used to teach the goal. Be sure that the group considers the role of the adult in its planning. The goals and activities developed could be shared with the larger group. Ask the groups why they chose the goal and the activities that they did. From the reports you can evaluate what material needs further explanation.

The case study described in Chapter 7 can also be used to illustrate how the process has been carried out and the results of the play tutoring done with one child. This serves as a model for those who do not understand the process and emphasizes how successful some of the strategies described can be.

Homework

Homework has been assigned for many of the classes that meet for more than one session. Between meetings participants are asked to observe one child in their setting and to complete the Play Checklist for her. For some, this is the first time that they have systematically observed an individual. Others who try to skip the observation and complete the checklist from memory recognize that without formally observing the child they have only partial information. They find that they must go back and observe in order to fill in the blanks.

Some participants become quite concerned about being able to complete the assignment. For these people it should be made clear that, unless you are in a formal educational setting, the purpose for their homework is not to evaluate them but to help them learn to use the Play Checklist.

Participants might also be asked to use the information from a checklist they have completed to write appropriate goals for the child they observed. Sometimes these goals are shared with another class member in order for the writer to receive feedback.

Group Brainstorms

Large group brainstorms can be used to draw from the expertise of the group. In a brainstorm the group is presented with a question and asked to list as many possible answers as they can think of. All answers are accepted during the brainstorming period. The answers that help to solve the problem or best demonstrate your point are emphasized.

Brainstorming has been used to help people think about many of the terms presented in the first chapter. After defining a term and giving some examples of what it looks like, you can ask participants to list the materials that they have in their settings which promote sensorimotor play or ask them to list some of the ways that adults and children interact.

Role-Playing

Role-playing is a valuable technique in which participants practice the strategies presented. However, adults vary greatly in their comfort level with playing a role in front of others. Use ice breakers consistently to build trust among group members to reduce the discomfort that some feel. In addition, it helps if the role plays are done in groups of three or four instead of in front of the entire group. This also makes it more likely that all participants will take on a role. Role plays can be helpful in trying out some of the roles of the adults and in learning to use some of the words suggested in solving conflicts and turn taking.

Disvoweled Terminology

In this activity, a number of terms are presented without vowels. Participants work in pairs or in small groups to identify the terms. For example:

PLY	=	PLAY
SCDRMTC	=	SOCIODRAMATIC
NSD TTRNG	=	INSIDE TUTORING

Adapted from Scannell and Newstrom, *More Games Trainers Play*, 1983.

Crossword Puzzle

A fun way to review some of the terms is to develop a simple crossword puzzle. This can be completed by small groups of participants, pairs, or individuals.

DIFFICULTIES

We have experienced some difficulties in meeting the needs of participants. We want to share with you a few of the things we have learned.

Information on play and the strategies for strengthening a child's play skills is needed by a variety of groups within the early childhood profession. Staff members from child care centers, family child care providers, special needs teachers, and preschool teachers may all be interested in this material. For this reason we use the terms "caregivers" and "adults" to refer to this broad group of educators. We also found that saying "your setting" or "your environment" was most acceptable as a descriptor of many early childhood environments.

If you are to use this material to train others effectively, it is important for you to have experience using the checklist. Complete the checklist for a number of children so that you know which of the areas are more difficult to observe. Use examples from your own experience teaching the skills needed for sociodramatic play to illustrate points in your presentation of the material.

If you plan to use the opening activity described earlier, be prepared to use the discoveries of the groups. This can be challenging as no two groups using the material will use them in the same way. Each time the activity is done it has a different outcome.

The description of the Play Checklist can seem quite theoretical to participants. When you present this information, be sure to break up the presentation so that people remain active in the discussion and so that they have opportunities to process it. Include some of the research on related topics. For instance, information on "popular" children can be presented during the discussion of interactions.

ENHANCERS

The material that is presented in this book is only a fraction of what is available on the topic of play. Depending on the level of the group you are working with and the time you have available you may want to enhance the material by including any of the following topics.

Arranging the Environment for Sociodramatic Play

Some suggestions for setting up sociodramatic play settings are included in Chapter 2. You might expand this by including a discussion of differing room arrangements and how they influence the behavior of children and can affect the level of play. You might also assign participants to change one aspect of their environment and note the effect it has on play.

Types of materials available for exploration and play might be a part of your discussion. List the materials that are available in most early childhood settings and how children use them.

Prop Boxes

The discussion of prop boxes can be expanded for those who have not used them. Brainstorm a list of possible themes for prop boxes. Have small groups decide which theme they want to work to develop. Each group should list:

props to be included in the boxes;
where this activity might take place in the room;
how you might extend the play to outdoors; and
what are some related activities that might go along with this theme.

The groups can make their lists on newsprint or transparencies to use in reporting back to the large group. Or, if you need an opportunity to move around, the lists can be displayed at each work area and the large group can walk around to each station and read what the small group has done.

Thematic Fantasy Play

Thematic fantasy play is another type of play training that an adult can use in teaching children about aspects of sociodramatic play. A well-known story is told and the children act out the parts of the characters. Stories that are repetitious are particularly good for this type of enactment. *Goldilocks and the Three Bears*, *Three Billy Goats Gruff*, and *The Carrot Seed* are favorites and lend themselves readily to this type of activity. (See the section on Role-Playing in Chapter 6.)

Children should know the story well before trying to use it in *thematic fantasy play*. They should be able to answer simple questions about the story line and the character's responses (Johnson, Christie, & Yawkey, 1987). In workshops, you may want caregivers to think of the types of questions that they would ask children in order to review the story and the types of props that might enhance the dramatization. Be sure to make the point that props should be limited so they do not become the focus of the activity. If too many props or props that require a great deal of manipulation are used, the children may become engrossed in working with them rather than on acting out the story (Johnson, Christie, & Yawkey, 1987).

Outdoor Play

Explore the sociodramatic play that takes place out of doors. Look at the types of play structures that enhance sociodramatic play. Or brainstorm how props and materials that are generally thought of as indoor toys may be used outdoors as well. Many caregivers think about setting up water play outdoors on a hot summer day. In addition, help caregivers think about setting up an outdoor grocery store or building a rocket ship on the playground. Using a balance beam out of doors or the bridge on a climber as the bridge in the *Three Billy Goats Gruff* might be a fun way to encourage children to play out roles.

Puppetry

Look at ways to use puppets in teaching children about the concepts presented in this material. Too often, all that children know how to do with puppets is to punch one another. Talk with the participants about how to use puppets and model stories for them to enact.

Spokesperson For Reality

A play training technique known as *spokesperson for reality* could be introduced. In this technique, play is momentarily suspended while the adult introduces reality to the play (Johnson, Christie, & Yawkey, 1987). For example, while the children are bathing dolls the adult might talk about and demonstrate how to towel dry and wrap a baby. Or, when a child is having difficulty getting along with another child, the adult might take one child aside and tell him, "Kaleb doesn't like it when you knock his tower down, but if you help him to build it up he might still want to play construction with you." One important thing to keep in mind with this technique is that it is quite disruptive to the ongoing play. Therefore, the children must be quite adept at resuming the play or the adult must take responsibility for getting the play going once again.

Extending play

You might also want to present ways to help children expand their play or to extend the length of time that they play one scenario. Talk about the types of materials that could be added to various interest areas in the setting. For example, after children have played a few days with office equipment, add a mailbox and a postal carrier's bag to keep children interested in this area.

In addition, discuss ways to extend an individual's interest in an activity. Brainstorm a list of the props that could be added to various play scenarios. Consider how to present the material so that the children are most likely to use it in their play. For example, when you see a group is starting to misuse the racing cars, suggest that they build a concession stand for the crowd at the races and sell cotton candy or popcorn. They could also build bleachers for the crowd to sit in.

APPENDIX 3

PLAY CHECKLIST and PLANNING FORM

PLAY CHECKLIST

Date: ______________________________

Name: ______________________________

Date of Birth: ______________________________

Check the highest level skills you consistently observe:

*1. Pretending with Objects
- ❑ Does not use objects to pretend
- ❑ Uses real objects
- ❑ Substitutes objects for other objects
- ❑ Uses imaginary objects

*2. Role-Playing
- ❑ No role play
- ❑ Uses one sequence of play
- ❑ Combines sequences
- ❑ Uses verbal declaration (i.e., "I'm a doctor.")
- ❑ Imitates actions of role, including dress

*3. Verbalizations about Play Scenario
- ❑ Does not use pretend words during play
- ❑ Uses words to describe substitute objects
- ❑ Uses words to describe imaginary objects and actions (i.e., "I'm painting a house.")
- ❑ Uses words to create a play scenario (i.e., "Let's say we're being taken by a monster.")

*4. Verbal Communication during a Play Episode
- ❑ Does not verbally communicate during play
- ❑ Talks during play only to self
- ❑ Talks only to adults in play
- ❑ Talks with peers in play by stepping outside of role
- ❑ Talks with peers from within role (i.e., "Eat your dinner before your dad comes home.")

*5. Persistence in Play
- ❑ Less than five minutes
- ❑ Six to nine minutes
- ❑ Ten minutes or longer

6. Interactions
- ❑ Plays alone
- ❑ Plays only with adults
- ❑ Plays with one child, always the same person
- ❑ Plays with one child, can be different partners
- ❑ Can play with two or three children all together

#7. Entrance to a Play Group
- ❑ Does not attempt to enter play group
- ❑ Uses force to enter play group
- ❑ Stands near group and watches
- ❑ Imitates behavior of group
- ❑ Makes comments related to play theme
- ❑ Gets attention of another child before commenting

8. Conflict Management
- ❑ Gives in during conflict
- ❑ Uses force to solve conflicts
- ❑ Seeks adult assistance
- ❑ Imitates verbal solutions provided by adults
- ❑ Recalls words to use when reminded
- ❑ Initiates use of words
- ❑ Accepts reasonable compromises

9. Turn-Taking
- ❑ Refuses to take turns
- ❑ Leaves toys: protests when others pick them up
- ❑ Gives up toy easily if done with it
- ❑ Gives up toy if another child asks for it
- ❑ Takes turns if arranged and directed by an adult
- ❑ Asks for turn, does not wait for a response
- ❑ Proposes turn taking; will take and give turns

10. Support of Peers
- ❑ Shows no interest in peers
- ❑ Directs attention to distress of peers
- ❑ Offers help
- ❑ Offers and takes suggestions of peers at times
- ❑ Encourages or praises peers

Note: The developmental progression outlined in each segment of the play checklist can be used as a guideline when assessing most children's development. However, not all individuals will go through the same steps in development nor through the same developmental sequence.

Sections marked with * are adapted from: Smilansky, S. 1968. *The Effects of Sociodramatic Play on Disadvantaged Preschool Children*. New York: Wiley

Sections marked with # are adapted from: Hazen, Black, & Fleming-Johnson. "Social Acceptance." *Young Children* 39 (1984): 26-36.

From *Pathways to Play: Developing Play Skills in Young Children*. Redleaf Press, 450 N. Syndicate, St. Paul, MN 55104, 1-800-423-8309.

PLANNING FORM

Child's Name: ______________________________

GOAL

Who: ______________________________

Does What: ______________________________

How well or how often: ______________________________

Target Completion Date for Goal: ______________________________

LESSON PLAN

Date: ______________________________

When will you work on the lesson? ______________________________

____

What are the child's special interests? ______________________________

____

How many children will be involved? ______________________________

____

Where will the playing take place? ______________________________

____

What props will be needed? ______________________________

____

Your role: ______________________________

____

Activities during play: ______________________________

____

____

Support Strategies: ______________________________

____

____

GLOSSARY

Associative Play: children play in the same area doing the same activity. They watch one another and imitate the actions of others but verbal exchanges are limited.

Auditory Cue: the signal a child hears that lets him know to stop or begin an action. A cue can be a verbal direction, a bell, a whistle, a clap, etc.

Autism, n., Autistic, adj.: a rare emotional disorder of childhood. A child with autism shows little response to outside reality and people and often has poor language development.

Co-playing: the adult joins play that is already started. Children remain in control of the play.

Cognitive Development: a child's ability to know, to be aware of objects, and to think, including understanding and reasoning.

Conflict Management: the ability to solve problems or disagreements with others.

Constructive Play: a child uses materials to make or build things.

Cooperative Play: two or more children organize and participate in play.

Current Level of Functioning: skills that a child is consistently capable of performing at the present time.

Developmental Assessment: a formal investigation of a child's skills to determine how his skills compare to those of other children the same age.

Developmental Checklist: an instrument that identifies the skills the child is currently demonstrating. It does not measure the developmental age of the child.

Disvoweled Terminology: an activity trainers use to review materials covered. Words are presented without the vowels. Participants fill in the vowels to identify the terms.

Dramatic Play: pretending with objects and roles to act out a scene.

Egocentric: self-centered. The way a child thinks about all things in terms of himself or how something affects him.

Empathy: the child's ability to put himself into another person's position and understand his feelings.

Free Choice: periods throughout the day when the child is allowed to choose how he will spend his time.

Games with Rules: a group of children agree upon rules to structure their play so that it can continue. Rules can be formal as in board games or informally agreed upon before play begins.

Ice Breakers: short exercises that help to build trust among group members. They help participants make informal contacts with one another.

Imitate: to copy an example or to repeat a word or behavior modeled.

Impulsive: to act suddenly or spontaneously. Sometimes appears as if the child can't stop himself from responding in certain ways.

Initiate: engages in or starts a behavior on his own.

Integrate: to fit into the group.

Interactions: the ways in which people are involved with one another.

Large Motor: the use of the large muscles of the body.

Lecturettes: short, formal presentations of information.

Manipulative: the ability to coordinate movements to move and to operate objects and materials.

Mentally Retarded: persons who are significantly below average in intelligence. They may need assistance learning independent living skills.

Objective: observable, without interpretation or judgement.

Observation: gaining a better understanding of a child's skill level by noting a fact or occurrence.

Parallel Play: 1) children play side by side with different activities and very little exchange of materials or conversation. 2) the adult plays next to the child.

Peers: people of approximately the same age.

Persistence: the ability to stick to a task for a certain amount of time.

Play Checklist: a tool developed to assist caregivers in their planning for an individual. To be used in teaching the skills that help a child to successfully engage in sociodramatic play.

Play Scenario: the play scene or story.

Play Tutoring: the adult begins the play and assumes partial control over the play. The adult teaches new play behaviors within the play episode.

Play Tutoring from Inside the Play: the adult takes on a role in play and becomes an active participant. The adult models many of the behaviors she wishes to teach.

Play Tutoring from Outside the Play: the adult does not join in the play but sits close by and makes comments and suggestions to the children.

Play with Objects: the ways in which a child uses toys and materials to discover and create.

Prompt: to give a cue or direction to get a behavior started.

Props: materials available to use in dramatic play. Enhance a child's ability to act out a role. May be replicas of real objects or substitutes for real objects.

Quantify: the ability to measure the number of behaviors listed in a goal.

Recall: to remember what has been modeled or taught.

Representational Skills: a child begins to use objects to pretend. The cognitive ability to have one item represent another.

Role-playing: when a child pretends to be someone other than himself. May be playing a role such as firefighter, parent, or waitress.

Self-Talk: a child talks to self, comments are not directed to another person.

Sensorimotor Play: the activities done by a child to explore the physical properties of toys or materials.

Sequence: an orderly succession of learning.

Social Play: play with others.

Sociodramatic Play: two or more children act out a play scenario. Children use roles, pretend with objects and actions, and communicate verbally from within the role for at least five minutes.

Solitary Play: child usually plays alone rather than with peers.

Speech Therapist: a specialist who identifies and works with people who have communication disorders.

Spokesperson for Reality: a play training technique in which play is momentarily suspended to introduce an element of reality into the play.

Strategies: plans for teaching which include activities and words to use.

Subjective: personal opinion. Interpretation and opinion is included in a description of a child's behavior.

Substance: a material or element such as water or sand.

Teachable Moments: spontaneously teaching when a child indicates interest in a topic or when a situation occurs.

Temperament: mode of emotional response typical of a particular child.

Thematic Fantasy Play: a well-known story is enacted by a group of children. Usually the adult narrates and keeps the story moving.

BIBLIOGRAPHY

Asher, S., P. Renshaw, and S. Hymel, "Peer Relations and the Development of Social Skills." In Moore, S. and Cooper, C., Ed. *The Young Child Reviews of Research.* Washington D.C.: NAEYC, 1982.

Beaty, Janice J. *Observing Development of the Young Child.* Columbus: Charles E. Merrill Publishing Company, 1986.

Burton and Woltag. *Pathways.* Menlo Park, CA: Addison-Wesley Publishing Company, 1986.

Chafel, J.A. and M.B. Childers, "Evaluating Children's Play Engagements for Social-Cognitive Growth." In McKee, J.S., Ed. *Play: Working Partner of Growth.* Maryland: Assn. for Childhood Education International, 1986.

Cherry, Clare. *Please Don't Sit on the Kids.* Belmont, CA: David S. Lake Publishers, 1983.

Cherry, Clare. *Think of Something Quiet.* Belmont, CA: Pitman Learning, Inc., 1981.

Christie, James F. "Sociodramatic Play Training." *Young Children* 37 (1982): 25-32.

Crary, Elizabeth. *Kids Can Cooperate.* Seattle: Parenting Press, Inc., 1984.

Crary, Elizabeth. *One Dozen Feeling Games.* Seattle: Parenting Press, 1980.

Crary, Elizabeth. *Without Spanking or Spoiling.* Seattle: Parenting Press, 1970.

Davis, Duane E. *My Friends and Me.* Circle Pines: American Guidance Service, Inc., 1977.

Derman-Sparks, Louise and the A.B.C. Task Force. *Anti-Bias Curriculum.* Washington D.C.: NAEYC, 1989.

Essa, Eva. *A Practical Guide to Solving Preschool Behavior Problems.* Albany: Delmar Publishers Inc., 1983.

Federlein, A. "Handicapped Preschoolers Mainstreamed in Play Based Classrooms Need Teachers Trained in Early Childhood and Special Education." *Index:Child Care* (1987):1-3.

Freyberg, J.T. "Increasing the Imaginative Play of Urban Disadvantaged Kindergarten Children Through Systematic Training." In J.L. Singer, Ed., *The Child's World of Make-Believe.* New York: Academic Press, 1973, pp. 129-154.

Golomb, Claire. "Pretense Play: A Cognitive Perspective." In Nancy R. Smith and Margery B. Franklin, Eds., *Symbolic Functioning in Childhood.* New Jersey: Lawrence Erlbaum Assn. Pub., 1979, pp. 101-116.

Halfin, Terry. "Play Training as an Intervention with Abused and Neglected Children." St. Mary's College: Unpublished, 1987.

Hatten, J. and P. Hatten, *Natural Language.* Arizona: Communication Skill Builders, Inc. 1981.

Hazen, Nancy, Betty Black, and Faye Fleming-Johnson. "Social Acceptance." *Young Children* 39 (1984): 26-36.

Heidemann, S. "Use of Objects in Symbolic Play by Special Needs Children." Wheelock College: Unpublished, 1981.

Howard, A. "Developmental Play Ages of Physically Abused and Nonabused Children." *The American Journal of Occupational Therapy* 40 (1986): 691-694.

Irwin, Eleanor C. "The Diagnostic and Theraputic Use of Pretend Play" in Schaefer and O'Connor, *Handbook of Play Therapy.* New York: John Wiley and Sons, 1983, pp.148-173.

Jennings, Mary. *Puppet Play Video.* Anew Dimension, 610 West 28th Street, Minneapolis, MN 55408, 1988.

Johnson, James E., James F. Christie, and Thomas D. Yawkey. *Play and Early Childhood Development.* Glenview, IL: Scott, Foresman and Co., 1987.

Katz, Lillian G. "The Professional Early Childhood Teacher." *Young Children* 39 (1984): 3-10.

Lindgren, Barbro. *Sam's Car.* New York: William Morrow and Company, 1982.

McDonald, J. and Y. Gillette, "Taking Turns: Teaching Communication to Your Child." *The Exceptional Parent* 15 (1985): 49-52.

Lamb, Gina. *Moving Machines Video.* Bo Peep Productions, P.O. Box 982, Eureka, MT, 59917, 1989.

Newstrom, John W. and Edward E. Scannell. *Games Trainers Play.* New York: McGraw Hill Book Company, 1980.

——*More Games Trainers Play.* New York: McGraw Hill Book Company, 1983.

Parten, M.B., "Social Participation Among Preschool Children." *Journal of Abnormal and Social Psychology* 27 (1932):243-269.

Piaget, J. *Play Dreams and Imitations.* New York: Norton, 1962.

Rice, Eve. *Sam Who Never Forgets.* New York: Greenwillow Books, 1977.

Rubin, Zick. *Children's Friendships.* Cambridge: Harvard University Press, 1980.

Smilansky, S. and Leah Shefatya. *Facilitating Play: A Medium for Promoting Cognitive, Socio-Emotional and Academic Development in Young Children.* Gaithersburg: Psychosocial & Educational Publications, 1990.

Smilansky, S. *The Effects of Sociodramatic Play on Disadvantaged Preschool Children.* New York: Wiley. 1968.

Mental Health Association of Minnesota *Very Important Kid.* Minneapolis: Mental Health Association of Minnesota 1989.

Vygotsky, L.S. "Play and Its Role in the Mental Development of the Child." In J.S. Bruner, A. Jolly, and K. Sylva (Eds.), *Play: Its Role in Development and Evolution.* New York: Basic Books, 1976, pp. 537-554.

Wing, L., J. Gould, S. Yeates, & L. Brierley, "Symbolic Play in Severely Mentally Retarded and in Autistic Children." *Journal of Child Psychology and Psychiatry* 18 (1977):167-178.

Wolfe, B., V. Petty, and K. McNellis. *Special Training for Special Needs.* Boston: Allyn and Bacon, 1990.

Wolfgang, Charles H., Bea Mackender, Mary E. Wolfgang. *Growing and Learning Through Play.* New York: McGraw Hill, 1981.

Wood, D., L. McMahon, and Y. Cranstoun. *Working with Under Fives.* Ypsilanti, MI: High/Scope Press, 1980.

Other Publications From Redleaf Press

Basic Guide to Family Child Care Record Keeping : Fourth Edition— Clear instructions on keeping necessary family day care business records.

Busy Fingers, Growing Minds — Over 200 original and traditional finger plays, with enriching activities for all parts of a curriculum.

Calendar-Keeper — Activities, family day care record keeping, recipes and more. Updated annually. Most popular publication in the field.

Calendario-Archivo—The *Calendar-Keeper* is now in Spanish!

Child Care Resource & Referral Counselors & Trainers Manual — Both a ready reference for the busy phone counselor and a training guide for resource and referral agencies.

Developing Roots & Wings: A Trainer's Guide to Affirming Culture In Early Childhood Programs — The training guide for Root & Wings, with 11 complete sessions and over 170 training activities.

The Dynamic Infant — Combines an overview of child development with innovative movement and sensory experiences for infants and toddlers.

Early Childhood Super Director — The first book of management strategies specifically for the early childhood director.

Family Child Care Contracts and Policies — Sample contracts and policies, and how - to information on using them effectively to improve tour business.

Family Child Care Tax Workbook — Updated every year, latest step-by-step information on forms, depreciation, etc.

Heart to Heart Caregiving: A Sourcebook of Family Day Care Activities, Projects and Practical Provider Support — Excellent ideas and guidance written by an experienced provider.

Kids Encyclopedia of Things to Make and Do — Nearly 2,000 art and craft projects for children aged 4-10.

The (No Leftovers!) Child Care Cookbook — Over 80 child-tested recipes and 20 menus suitable for family child care providers and center programs. CACFP creditable.

Open the Door, Let's Explore — Full of fun, inexpensive neighborhood walks and field trips designed to help young children.

Practical Solutions to Practically Every Problem: The Early Childhood Teacher's Manual — Over 300 proven developmentally appropriate solutions for all kinds of classroom problems.

Roots & Wings: Affirming Culture in Early Childhood Programs — A new approach to multicultural education that helps shape positive attitudes toward cultural differences.

Sharing in the Caring — Packet to help establish good relationships between providers and parents with agreement forms and other information.

Snail Trails and Tadpole Tails — A fun nature curriculum with five easy-to-do, hands on units that explore the lifecycle of these intriguing creatures: snails, worms, frogs, praying mantises and worms.

Staff Orientation in Early Childhood Programs — Complete manual for orienting new staff on all program areas.

Teachables From Trashables — Step-by-step guide to making over 50 fun toys from recycled household junk.

Teachables II — Similar to *Teachables From Trashables*; with another 75-plus toys.

Those Mean Nasty Dirty Downright Disgusting but... Invisible Germs — A delightful story that reinforces for children the benefits of frequent hand washing.

Trusting Toddlers: Planning for One to Three Year Olds in Child Care Centers — Expert panel explains how to set up toddler programs that really work.

CALL FOR CATALOG OR ORDERING INFORMATION
1-800-423-8309